Call to
all
to
Prayer

A Season of Harvest

STANDARD
PUBLISHING
Cincinnati, Ohio

Cover design by SchultzWard, Inc.

The Standard Publishing Company, Cincinnati, Ohio.
A division of Standex International Corporation.

00 99 98 97 96 95 94 93   5 4 3 2 1

Library of Congress Cataloging-in-Publication Data

A Call to prayer : a season of harvest
      p. cm.
   ISBN 0-87403-999-1
   1. Prayer.
  BV213.C35   1993
  248.3'2--dc20   93-4072
                                     CIP

Contents

Introduction

David Butts, Senior Minister of the Kansas Christian Church, Kansas, IL; Prayer Chairman of a national task force on missions; Compiler of this book

Many books have been written on prayer. So why another? Perhaps it is not so much the content as the timing that sets this book apart from others. It follows a national and international Call to Prayer issued by a number of Christians. Implementing the prayer ideas within this book can give further impetus to this prayer movement.

The Call to Prayer is a challenge to become people of prayer. It is a challenge to covenant or promise to pray especially about awakening and world evangelization. Many have already signed the covenant of prayer. Will you covenant to join other Christians across America and around the world in a SEASON OF PRAYER?

This call for Christians to pray had a simple beginning. A group discussing how to plant churches and grow them came to this conclusion: "Let's pray and let's encourage others to pray with us, and God will direct his church."

This SEASON OF PRAYER is an attempt to seek God's guidance as people look for ways to be involved in fulfilling his mission.

Can we unite in prayer? Think of what could happen—churches setting aside additional time for prayer, Bible colleges uniting in a day of prayer, missionaries praying for their home church, leaders praying for vision, and everyone praying for renewed awareness of church planting, church growth, and teaching. Who knows what the Holy Spirit can yet accomplish through his people?

Awakening! This is what can happen if we will pray.

Will you covenant to pray? Will you covenant to use your influence and level of responsibility in our Lord's church to urge and encourage people to pray? Would you ask others to join you in this covenant?

Jesus said, "Ask the Lord of the harvest . . . to send out workers" (Luke 10:2). What a promise!

Ready to accept the challenge? The challenge is to pray with power and passion about the great biblical themes of revival and of world evangelization.

I want to express my appreciation to the individual authors for their willingness to share what they have learned about prayer with the rest of us. They are all busy people with fruitful ministries, but they took the time to write from their hearts because they know the value of prayer. The greatest thanks you could give them would be not just to read the book, but to pray your way through it. That would make it well worth their time.

Many people desire to pray but feel they lack the practical knowledge to be true men and women of prayer. The prayer of the authors is that the following chapters will give the kind of practical help you need to become a prayer warrior, one whom God can use to change this world.

The Power of Prayer

Knofel Staton, Chancellor and Professor of New Testament at Pacific Christian College, Fullerton, California

Prayer meetings are not in fashion these days, are they? Remember when the midweek service used to be a prayer service? The whole meeting focused on prayer, with nearly everyone who attended participating. There was at least forty-five minutes of prayer.

Then those meetings began to change. Music was added. The result? Thirty-five minutes of prayer and ten minutes of music. We added a meditation. The result? Ten minutes of meditation or a devotional, ten minutes of music, and twenty-five minutes of prayer. Then came special music. The result? Ten minutes of meditation, five minutes of special music, ten minutes of congregational music, and twenty minutes of prayer. Then the meditation was replaced with a Bible study. The result? Ten minutes of congregational music, five minutes of special music, twenty minutes of Bible study, and ten minutes of prayer.

Then the Bible study was expanded—so much so that the midweek service was now called a Bible study rather than a prayer meeting. The result? Thirty-five minutes of Bible study, five to ten minutes of music, and opening and closing prayers. Total prayer time? Now less than one minute.

Call the church to a special prayer meeting any day or night of the week and see what happens attendance-wise. Call the church to a special music concert and see what happens attendance-wise.

Who waits upon the Lord today—when someone can make a motion, someone else can second it, and the majority can pass it? Anybody for putting off a vote and entering into a season of prayer to wait for an evident intervention of God?

Christianity in America, which has put prayer on the back burner, is not the Christianity of most of Christ's followers around the world. Is it possible that we have become so self-sufficient in this country that we think we don't need God's supremacy? Is it possible that as long as things are going well, we think, "God, why don't you go somewhere else where you're really needed? When we really need you, we will call upon you. OK? We don't want to unnecessarily wear you out, involve you, or cause you to divert your attention from those who really need you. We're getting along OK. Thank you, God."

Who really needs God? If we get sick, we can call the doctor or go to the emergency room. If a natural calamity destroys our property, we can fill out an insurance claim. If company comes unexpectedly and we're short on food, we can go to the supermarket. If we run out of money, we can use the plastic card. If we don't have enough to make ends meet, we can get food stamps or a loan. If we are having relational difficulties, we can go to a counselor. If our clothes wear out, we can go to a clothing store. If we want to know what to do in church programming, we can always check how others do it, present it to the committee, and take a vote.

When we are asked to pray for people in various situations during worship services or Sunday school classes, are we really interested and involved enough to pray for them during the week? Some of us may take notes during the sermon time, but how many take note of the prayer requests? Do we believe everyone else is going to be praying, so God doesn't need our prayers? Or could it be that we don't intend to be a people of prayer during the week? If that is so, do we really believe that God is a prayer-hearing and a prayer-answering God?

Have we come to believe that God has quit doing any miracles after the New Testament was written, or after the apostles all died? Have we de-powered God in our theology and teaching? If so, we have become Christian humanists who believe that we humans can do anything if we take the time to plan carefully and implement the plan—and that God no longer has the power he had in Bible times.

In Woody Allen's *Love and Death*, Napoleon walked by his lady's room and heard voices. "I was praying," the lady explained.

"But I heard two voices," Napoleon said.

"I do both parts," she replied.

Is that what we do—both parts? We talk to God and then decide what his answer will be and should be. If we decide that he can't or won't answer, we just don't pray.

But people don't pray because they believe in prayer. They pray because they believe in God. If people do believe that he is the all-powerful God of the Bible, who has not put his power on hold—then they will pray.

The power of prayer is the power of God. His inspired Word declares, "Our God is in heaven; he does whatever pleases him" (Psalm 115:3). God does whatever he pleases, and he doesn't need our vote—nor does he wait for our veto. He declared to his people, "I will do all that I please" (Isaiah 46:10).

Even Nebuchadnezzar knew that the God of Israel had that kind of power, for he declared,

He does as he pleases
  with the powers of heaven
  and the peoples of the earth.
No one can hold back his hand
  or say to him: "What have you done?" (Daniel 4:35).

Our need is not for a lesson about prayer but for a lesson on the awesomeness of God. Many of us have been taught that the only reason we pray is to change ourselves. But the Bible does not teach that as a reason to pray. Instead the Bible teaches that prayer affects God and that prayer can affect circumstances.

Prayer Affects God

Aren't you affected when your kids talk with you? Of course you are. And so is God. He is the perfect parent as well as the powerful creator. The Bible teaches that God is affected when his people pray.

For instance, remember when God brought his people out of Egypt through those great miracles? After coming through the sea, God's people stopped at Mt. Sinai for a time. While Moses was having a long talk with God on the mountain, God's people got impatient. They took off their jewelry, melted it down, poured the liquid into a mold shaped like a calf—and guess what resulted? A golden calf! Then they worshiped that calf, sang hymns to that calf, brought offerings to that calf, and declared that the calf was the god who had brought them out of Egypt.

That ticked God off. He said to Moses, "I have seen these people . . . and they are a stiff-necked people." Then God gave Moses a command: "Now leave me alone. . . ." (Have you ever said anything like that to your kids?) God continued, ". . . so that my anger may burn against them and that I may destroy them. Then I will make you into a great nation" (Exodus 32:9, 10).

Even though God told Moses to leave him alone, Moses immediately began to beg God not to destroy his people (Exodus 32:11-13). He kept begging for forty days and forty nights (Deuteronomy 9:18). Do you know what happened? "The Lord relented and did not bring on his people the disaster he had threatened (Exodus 32:14).

Isn't it marvelous that our prayers can make a difference with God? God listened carefully and changed his mind.

And then there was King Hezekiah. God told Hezekiah through the prophet Isaiah to get his house in order because he was going to die (2 Kings 20:1). But Hezekiah prayed to the Lord, and before Isaiah got out of town, God told him to go back and tell the king, "I have heard your prayer and seen your tears; I will heal you. . . . I will add fifteen years to your life" (2 Kings 20:5, 6).

Some people suggest that God never changes his mind, but listen to what God says about himself. God's own understanding about what he will do is better than any theologian's understanding. God says, "If at any time I announce that a nation or kingdom is to be uprooted, torn down and destroyed, and if that nation I warned repents of its evil, then I will relent and not inflict on it the disaster I had planned" (Jeremiah 18:7, 8).

While God will never change his mission, his goal, or his plan for the redemption of humanity, he will and can change some particulars and methods in response to the prayers of his children. That's part of what it means to be God. He has that right, and he has demonstrated that many times in the Bible. For us to say that God will not or can not do that is for us to freeze God's flexibility and to paralyze his power.

Prayer Can Affect Circumstances

Prayer can affect circumstances because we are talking to the one who has all power. Then, today, and forever. One of the messages of the Bible is the all-powerfulness of God. In Genesis, we read, "Is anything too hard for the Lord?" (18:14). God himself asked his people, "Is the Lord's arm too short?" (Numbers 11:23). When God was going to fill a valley full of water without any rain or wind, He said, "This is an easy thing in the eyes of the Lord" (2 Kings 3:18). The prophet declares that nothing is too hard for God (Jeremiah 32:17). An angel that came directly from Heaven to Mary brought this message: "Nothing is impossible with God" (Luke 1:37). Jesus, who knows God better than anyone, said, "With God all things are possible" (Matthew 19:26).

If God, an angel, an inspired prophet, and Jesus affirm the all-powerfulness of God, then we who are Christians ought to catch on to that kind of thinking!

No wonder the psalmist declared that God is an awesome God (Psalm 47:2, 89:7, 99:3, 111:9). Job declared that God does great things beyond our understanding (Job 5:9).

I used to believe that all of life on earth was controlled by natural laws, but I was mistaken. There is no such thing as natural law—as if all such laws belonged to nature. They are all supra-natural laws. They were created by God and belong to God—gravitation, laws of thermodynamics, speed of light, etc. The Bible is clear on that point. Either we believe in the God of creation or we affirm some kind of accidental evolution. If we believe in the God of creation, that same God has the same power today.

The inspired psalmist, discussing natural phenomena, declared that when God sends a command to the earth, what he says is quickly done (Psalm 147:15). Even the sun, the moon, and the stars cannot disobey him (Psalm 148:6). No wonder the psalmist said that our Lord is in Heaven and does whatever he pleases, for all of nature belongs to him. He can intervene in those laws he created any time he wants to, and for any reason he wants to, without getting anything else in nature out of balance.

The disciples once asked each other about Jesus, "Who is this? He commands even the winds and the water, and they obey him" (Luke 8:25). When Jesus commanded that the fig tree dry up, it did not have a committee meeting with the other fig trees to see what to do. Any time God speaks to nature, nature has no option but to obey immediately.

We human beings are the only part of creation that God has given the freedom to listen to a command and then decide whether to obey or not. Nothing else has that option. That's the reason God could say to the Red Sea, "Open up," and the sea opened up. While some may say it was a wind that drove the waters of the sea back, God declared, "By a mere rebuke I dry up the sea" (Isaiah 50:2).

Remember the battle Joshua was involved in? Daylight was running out before the battle was. Joshua prayed for more daylight. If I were Joshua, I would've asked for a quick victory; but Joshua evidently liked to fight more than I do. The Bible says God caused the sun to stand still. What a day that was!

Some people say that shows the Bible does not know anything about science, because it's not the sun that moves but the earth. I believe God knew that. I suspect God said something like this: "Earth, stop right now in your tracks—and everything else that is dependent on the earth's rotation, just hang loose. I'm in charge here." Don't let the phrase "the sun stood still" bother your confidence in God's knowledge. I guarantee you the next time you watch the weather on television, you will see "Sunrise at 7:10" or "Sunset at 8:35." I've never heard anyone say, "I'm never gonna watch that television network again because they should scientifically say, 'Tomorrow morning the earth is going to rotate so that edge of the circumference of the sun will appear on the horizon at 7:10 A.M." Who wants to hear all that, when "sunrise" and "sunset" communicates to us?

Remember when Daniel was thrown to the lions? The lions were starving, but when Daniel came on the scene, God must have said, "Right now, lions, you have anorexia." Those lions lost their appetite.

Remember when Jonah was thrown overboard? The Bible says that God provided a great fish to swallow him (Jonah 1:17). God must have said, "Now, fish, the very next thing you see splash into the water, swallow it whole but don't hurt it." That fish had no option but to obey.

Jonah was in that fish for three days and three nights. I'm convinced he tried every way he could to get out—yelled, tickled the ribs (or whatever was on the inside of the fish)—but nothing worked. Jonah finally realized that he was in a crisis and started to pray. Aren't we often the same way? As soon as Jonah finished praying, "the Lord ordered the fish to spit Jonah up onto the beach, and it did" (Jonah 2:10, TEV). God must have said, "Now, fish, I want you to surface and find the beach and spit that man out onto the beach." That must have been one fantastic spit!

The power of prayer is the power of the God to whom we talk.

What About Today?

Our God is the same yesterday, today, and forever. One of the things that is the same is his power. It is the arrogance of man—our philosophy of independence, our self-sufficiency—that teaches that God checked in his power at the end of the first century. Not a hint in the Bible suggests that.

I am convinced that we have caved in to that theology because we like to stay in control ourselves—so we replace prayer with planning, intercession with involvement, waiting with working, patience with perspiration. We have made organizational skills and planning more significant than God's power. We have given more power to the church's bylaws and constitution than we have to the creator's ongoing and consistent ability.

Does God really continue to hear our prayers and intervene in our lives today? Of course he does.

Many of our missionaries observe God's intervention firsthand, but tragically, when they come home they cannot talk about the powerful workings of God, lest we become too uncomfortable and withdraw our support.

Ron Morse witnessed an example of God's intervention years ago. He was working with some villagers in northern Thailand. That area was having the worst grasshopper plague they could remember. The leader of the village said to Ron, "You go away and gather your Christians and pray for three weeks that the grasshoppers will leave the Christians' fields but not the non-Christians' fields. If when you return in three weeks, the grasshoppers have left the Christians' fields and are still in the non-Christians' fields, I will help you lead this whole village to worship your Jesus." What a challenge!

With earnestness and sincerity, the Christians prayed. Three weeks later Ron came into the village and was devastated by what he saw. It was obvious that the grasshoppers were still in the Christians' fields. In fact, there were more grasshoppers in those fields. But upon more careful examination, they found that the grasshoppers in the Christians' fields were only eating the weeds—they were not touching the rice—while the grasshoppers in the non-Christians' fields were eating the rice and not the weeds. There were so many grasshoppers in the Christians' fields that the dung they left fertilized the ground, so that there was an abundance of rice to feed the people. We have an awesome God!

Missionary Jim McElroy tells about what happened in the Philippines when he was called into a village. An infant was deathly ill. The child had not nursed for days and was turning gray. His eyes were rolled back; he was lifeless and listless, just moments from death.

Jim turned to the Filipino preacher and said, "I did not know we were coming here for a medical reason. I brought no medicine. Did you?"

The Filipino preacher said no.

"What shall we do?" Jim asked.

"Let's just pray."

While they were praying fervently for God's intervention, the little infant reached up and touched one of those who was praying. Before they finished, the infant moved toward the mother's breast and began to nurse.

The following Sunday was Easter. As Jim was preaching in a neighboring village in an outdoor assembly, he saw coming over the brink of the hill a woman carrying a baby. Behind her were over twenty adults. As they got closer, Jim recognized the mother and the infant, who was looking very healthy. The adults had come to accept Jesus Christ and to be immersed. We serve a powerful and awesome God!

That does not mean God will always answer our prayers in the affirmative or always intervene. We have all experienced the "no" answers. We must be careful if we start to believe that we can order God around with our prayers. God does not honor the "name it and claim it" game some people play—as if they can tell God what to do.

The prophet declared, "Who can speak and have it happen if the Lord has not decreed it?" (Lamentations 3:37). Our God listens carefully to our petitions, prayers, intercessions, agonies, heartaches, and persistent begging. But he will not permit us to dictate to him what he has to do.

How do we understand it when we pray for someone to be healed and that person dies? It does not mean that God loves some more and some less, or that God respects some and not others. "As high as the heavens are above the earth, so great is his love for those who fear him" (Psalm 103:11). With that great love, he also declares,

> My thoughts are not your thoughts,
>   neither are your ways my ways . . .
> As the heavens are higher than the earth,
>   so are my ways higher than your ways
>   and my thoughts than your thoughts (Isaiah 55:8, 9).

I believe we can trust in a God who is that big and has that much love for us.

When the answer does not come exactly the way we want or expect, our faith should hold hands with the faith of those three chaps thrown in the furnace of fire, who declared, "If we are thrown into the blazing furnace, the God we serve is able to save us from it, and he will rescue us from your hand . . . But even if he does not, we want you to know . . . that we will not serve your gods or worship the image of gold you have set up" (Daniel 3:17).

Our trust in the power of God continues not because we always get our way, but because we believe in the way of God!

To pray is to tap into God's power. Non-Christians do not believe that God still has power today. If Christians don't believe it, who will? Isn't it time for us to catch up with our forefathers and believe in, teach about, and pray to the kind of God we read about in Ephesians 3:20, "who is able to do . . . all that we ask or think"? We can think of great things. Wouldn't a God who could accomplish all of them be a great God?

But that's not what Ephesians 3:20 says. Such a God is too small.

Did Paul write, "Now to him who is able to do *beyond* all that we ask or think"? That God is too small. Did he write, "Now to him who is able to do *abundantly beyond* all that we ask or think"? Even that God is too small. Here's what Paul wrote: "Now to Him who is able to do exceeding abundantly beyond all that we ask or think, according to the power that works within us, to Him be the glory in the church and in Christ Jesus to all generations forever and ever. Amen." (Ephesians 3:20, 21, NASB)

That's the power of prayer. It is tapping into him who is able to do exceeding—abundantly—beyond—all—that we can possibly ask or think. What a God and what a privilege—to actually talk with him, and know that he listens.

Questions for Discussion

1. Why has the prayer meeting been replaced by Bible studies? How can the goals of both the prayer meeting and the Bible study be met without compromising either?

2. Is affluence necessarily a hindrance to depending on God? If so, why? If not, how can one maintain dependence on God in spite of affluence?

3. The author cites several instances where God apparently changed his mind. Yet 1 Samuel 15:29 declares that God "does not lie or change his mind; for he is not a man that he should change his mind." How does this affect your understanding of prayer?

4. How does Jesus' power over nature while he walked this earth suggest his ability to answer prayers today?

5. Why do modern Christians seem to believe God does not act with the same power as he did in the days recorded in the Bible? Is there some difference between the means God used to act then and the means he uses now? If so, what?

6. What answers to prayer have you experienced? How did the experience affect your faith?

7. How does a "no" answer to prayer affect your faith? In what ways can it build your faith?

You Can Pray Without Hypocrisy:

The Model Prayer

E. LeRoy Lawson, President of Pacific Christian College, Fullerton, CA; Pastor of Central Christian Church, Mesa, AZ

If it weren't for Jesus' down-to-earth, right-to-the-point model prayer (Matthew 6:5-15), I wouldn't have the nerve to write this chapter. I'd feel too hypocritical. Mine is not an exemplary prayer life. Prayer meetings often depress me. Experienced participants utter their petitions with such eloquence and sincerity and at such length that I feel, well, outclassed. How dare I presume?

Jesus' brief prayer gives me license to try, inept as I am. According to Jesus, you don't have to be schooled in the subtleties of the truly religious to pray. You just have to want to talk with God, honestly, without ostentation.

As a matter of fact, strutting your spirituality is the very thing that turns Jesus off. He nestles his comments on prayer between his guidelines for charity to the needy and for fasting. Concerning each of these three "acts of righteousness" the word is the same: don't strut your stuff (Matthew 6:1).

Religion's not for show. Playactors (hypocrites) perform for the crowd. Too bad for them. They've chosen the wrong audience. They can lavish their alms, fast themselves haggard, and flaunt their supplications in synagogue and on street corner, but the only applause they'll hear is from their own kind. God won't be attending their performances. He could tell they weren't meant for him. What the actors wanted was to catch people's attention, Jesus says, and they got what they desired. Too bad they weren't more interested in God's opinion.

Jesus isn't saying anything in his sermon that hadn't already been taught in Scripture. He must have caught his disciples' attention, though, since their erstwhile spiritual superiors seemed to have been for everything Jesus is against. They had forgotten Ecclesiastes 5:1-3.

> Guard your steps when you go to the house of God. Go near to listen rather than to offer the sacrifice of fools, who do not know that they do wrong.
> Do not be quick with your mouth,
>> do not be hasty in your heart
>> to utter anything before God.
> God is in heaven
>> and you are on earth,
>> so let your words be few.
> As a dream comes when there are many cares,
>> so the speech of a fool when there are many words.

Like the Preacher, Jesus warns against parading instead of praying.

It's instructive to note what Jesus ignores in his sermon. He is indifferent to form and posture. He doesn't prescribe kneeling or standing or sitting or prostrating oneself; his silence suggests that the body's bearing has little to do with the prayer's effectiveness. Like other Bible voices (except when dealing with public worship), Jesus doesn't dictate the time or place or physical attitude to be assumed when talking with God. In the Scriptures, standing seems to be commonplace, although kneeling (and even prostrating oneself) is mentioned. Hands were spread and lifted heavenward sometimes; at other times they beat the breast in penitence. Sweat and tears were not strangers to the petitioner. Bible writers apparently took it for granted that in genuine prayer, body language complements the verbal communication.

In cautioning against hypocrisy, Jesus urges his disciples to center their thoughts on God, for only he can give the reward they should seek. To do so, privacy helps; in our closets we aren't tempted to swagger. Before the living God, brevity, not verbosity, commends us. "Babbling," he calls this tendency of ours to pile up paragraphs in the hope that, failing to sway God in any other way, we can verbally pommel him into submitting to our entreaties. Such overkill is entirely inappropriate, Jesus contends, since "your Father knows what you need before you ask him."

How then shall we pray?

Personal

God is our "Father." Once we have accepted this relationship, we can relax. One doesn't posture before one's father. At least not for very long.

When I sat for my oral examination in my doctoral program, I was as nervous as I have ever been in my life. There they were, five professors representing all of English and American literature, ready to probe my limited grasp of this huge field to find my weaknesses. They could ask me anything they wanted, from the beginning of the English language to the most recent scholarly publication. And I was supposed to be able to answer.

On the team was my major professor. He was the leadoff examiner and, sensing my extreme anxiety, he kindly tried to ease me into the inquisition with a very simple question. Could I please give him some of the Anglo-Saxon words for God? I was so rattled I couldn't name any, including GOD. It was not my finest hour.

My finest hours in praying, though, come when I do remember my favorite biblical name for God. It's the one Jesus permits—nay, encourages—us to use. He is Father. Like a prodigal son racing home from his dalliance with the pigs, I come ashamed but nearly desperate for the embrace of my Father. I don't deserve it, but I know I'm lost without it. And when I'm with him, I am a better person. This is why, as Paul urges, I need to pray without ceasing. Without praying, I cease being the person the prayer evokes.

Submissive

Don't misunderstand. To call him Father is not to intrude. He's still our Father "in Heaven." We "come into his presence"; we don't cozy up. We haven't become buddies. There is still the respectful distance, the seeking to know his sometimes inscrutable will, the ever-present consciousness of his holiness and our unworthiness. We know something of his mind, but only as much as he has revealed of it. We don't pretend to be his peers. Ours is not a club of equals.

That's why we recall the "in heaven" part of the prayer. It reminds us we don't live where he lives; he remains the Lord, high and lifted up, even as we thank his Spirit for indwelling us. He is always more than a mere "voice within." G.K. Chesterton rightly grumbled, "That Jones shall worship the god within him turns out ultimately that Jones shall worship Jones." God forbid.

He is, even in our intimate moments with him, "O Lord most holy."

Discerning

"Hallowed be your name," Jesus teaches us to address our Father. It's the lesson the prodigal learned. He had tried writing his father out of his life's script. He could do it better his way. He had taken his inheritance and squandered it on the good life. He had immersed himself in the best the world offers. He had drunk its wine and sung its songs and had its women. When he sobered up in the pig sty, he was forced to admit there was only one abode where he really belonged. It was a sanctified place, special to him because his father dwelt there. His father was unlike anyone else he had encountered in his truancy, and his father's example and instruction towered above all other philosophies and so-called "truths" he had heard in his wanderings. There was about his father an aura, a difference—a holiness. He now revered his father's name as never before. His errant odyssey had convinced him. He could now intelligently, experientially discern the difference between his unique father and everyone else. Whom he formerly despised and couldn't wait to escape he now returned to in utter repentance. He had discovered what was worth hallowing.

Prioritizing

Forgive my use of this ugly word. I'm employing it because of its popularity, not its beauty. I'm still thinking of the prodigal son. After he discerned his father's uniqueness, he was ready to do whatever his father asked him. Not daring to ask for his former place at the family table, he was willing to be a servant, if only he could live on his father's holdings. He was finished with demanding his rights, doing things his way, playing his own god. His new speech had become, "Your kingdom come, your will be done."

Earlier, the son had wanted only the father's money. Now he wanted to do his will.

Will Herberg once observed that contemporary American religiosity converts God into "a great cosmic public utility." He is useful for getting what we want. This divine public servant helps us to get our kingdom to come and our will to be done.

With the parallel lines so popular in Hebrew poetry, in which the second line repeats what the first has already said, Jesus equates "your kingdom come" and "your will be done." The kingdom of God exists wherever his will is supreme.

This isn't an easy petition. *Kingdom* is an exotic term for us. They had kingdoms in the old country, but this is America, a democracy, where everyone is equal to everyone else. Back then our ancestors pioneered this land to get away from a king, and we don't intend to tolerate one now. Our leader is merely Mr. President, thank you, and woe to any pretender who forgets that.

In our prodigal stage, we just as passionately resist a God who acts like God. We want the inheritance, all right, but we can do without the obedience stuff. We can do it just fine without any divine authority. Like the prodigal son, however, we can only begin to find real life when we're ready to submit. "Your will be done" then means, "I personally intend to do your will."

There are several other possible meanings, all less than satisfactory:

Resignation is one. "Whatever will be will be" is a popular wording of this attitude. It's a stoic acceptance of the inevitable. Sometimes it sounds a little like the petulant teenager who finally gives in. "OK, have it your way."

Resentment is another. "You win, you win" is what's verbalized while the silent mind mutters, "But I don't like it and I don't have to like it and I won't forget you made me do it." Algernon Swinburne put it into verse:

Thou hast conquered, O pale Galilean;
The world has grown gray from thy breath.

Simple *trust* is also expressed in "thy will be done." John Greenleaf Whittier says it for many of us:

I know not where his islands lift
    Their fronded palms in air.

I only know I cannot drift
        Beyond his love and care.

Active participation is implicit in Jesus' prayer, though. "I want it to be done your way, Father. Even more, I want to do it your way." When Jesus prayed in Gethsemane, "Yet not as I will, but as you will," he was expressing neither resignation nor resentment, but trust and active participation. He would let the Father's will be done through him and would do whatever he must to bring it to fulfillment.

Jesus would not have taught us to ask, "Your will be done," if it always were. In Heaven things go God's way, but not on earth. Order prevails there; here, disorder. It has been so since just after the beginning, when Adam and Eve asserted themselves, granting their will a higher priority than his. What are we to conclude from the accounts of Noah and the flood, the Israelites' extended sojourn in the wilderness, the corruption in the Corinthian church, the prophetic indictments against the faithless people of God in the Old Testament or the pitiful churches in the book of Revelation in the New, if not that God doesn't always (or even usually) get his way on earth? Our prayer, then, is to make ourselves instruments of his benevolent desires on earth, to team up with him against the countervailing forces of evil. We can make a difference. If we would, we could still make the kind of impact that caused one seventeenth-century secularist to moan, "I had rather meet coming against me a whole regiment with drawn swords than one Calvinist convinced that he is doing the will of God."

We can be like Robert Morrison, the famed missionary who, when preparing to embark for his commissioned duties in China, was chided by his ship's owner, "And so, Mr. Morrison, you really expect that you will make an impression on the idolatry of the great Chinese empire?"

"No sir," Morrison replied. "I expect God will."

God would do it. But Morrison would help. He would be an instrument of God's will on earth. That was his top priority.

Humble

"Give us today our daily bread." We don't ask for more. We trust you, Father, for today's requirements. We don't demand a well-stocked pantry. Nor are luxuries on our list. Just enough for today. We'll be back tomorrow to ask you about tomorrow.

This is the first petition in the brief prayer that is directly for ourselves. Jesus' disciples must have thought of their forefathers roaming the wilderness, dependent on God's daily portion of manna (Exodus 16:1-21). It was all that separated them from starvation, yet they were forbidden to put something away for the next day.

Jesus returns to the theme in the Sermon on the Mount, Matthew 6:25-34, allaying fears about tomorrow's menu or worries about today's thirsts. Such fretting is the mark of paganism. Since nonbelievers have no higher source of power or provision, they naturally devote their energies to buying and getting and storing and adorning. Jesus' followers, knowing that "in all things God works for the good of those who love him, who have been called according to his purpose" (Romans 8:28) have nothing to worry about in regard to these essentials. God knows what we need. And he provides for those who humbly wait on his grace.

Fair

I read somewhere many years ago that Beau Jack (Sidney Walker), the illiterate Augusta, Georgia, shoeshine boy who boxed his way to the world lightweight boxing championship, was noted for praying before every fight. When asked whether he prayed for the Lord to help him win, he said, "No. Suppose I pray to win. The other boy, he prayed to win, too. Then what God gonna do?" So he prayed nobody would get hurt and that it would be a good fight. That was enough.

Beau Jack was fair in his fighting and fair in his praying. Fairness is something Jesus values, also.

Forgive us our debts,
as we also have forgiven our debtors.

It's an unexpected twist, isn't it? Who doesn't demand fairness in life—for himself, that is? But when the scale tips in our favor, is it fairness we want, or justice? Or even vengeance, like the angry woman who spoke to me following a morning service, livid with Chrysler Corporation for foisting a faulty automobile on her. She didn't want revenge, she assured me, shaking her fist, but justice! (I thought of Shakespeare's line, "The lady doth protest too much, methinks.") She was in no mood to hear anything about forgiveness. She spoke of justice, but nothing less than vengeance could temper her temper.

She wouldn't have listened to any such words from Jesus, either. Had I thought of it, I might have tried Epictetus, the pre-Christian philosopher. Not that she'd have heard of him, I suppose, but I have found it enlightening that this non-Christian thinker agrees with Jesus in urging the aggrieved party to forgive. His little dialogue says it all:

My brother ought not to have treated me thus.
True: but he must see to that. However he may treat me, I must deal rightly by him. This is what lies with me, what none can hinder.[1]

The poet John Dryden agrees: "Forgiveness to the injured doth belong."

Why should the injured party have to take the initiative?

Because the ailing relationship matters more than any particular hurt, which makes forgiveness an even larger matter than merely overlooking this debt or that slight. As Voltaire pointed out a long time ago, "To forgive our enemies their virtues—that is a greater miracle." And to forgive another for one's own sake, well, as Jane Merchant has noted,

If I forgive an injury
Because resenting would poison me—
I may feel noble, I may feel splendid,
But it isn't exactly what Christ intended.[2]

There's a toughness about Jesus' expectation, isn't there? Just how tough is spelled out in Matthew 18:23-35, where Jesus promises a grim future for an unforgiving person. "In anger his master turned him over to the jailers until he should pay back all he owed" (v. 34).

It's only fair. When General Oglethorpe told John Wesley he never forgave, Wesley retorted, "Then I hope, sir, you never sin." Wesley knew something of God's fairness.

Honest

Jesus would have us pray, "Lead us not into temptation," but James contends that God doesn't ever tempt us:

> When tempted, no one should say, "God is tempting me." For God cannot be tempted by evil, nor does he tempt anyone; but each one is tempted when, by his own evil desire, he is dragged away and enticed. Then, after desire has conceived, it gives birth to sin; and sin, when it is full-grown, gives birth to death (James 1:13-15).

Why, then, does Jesus tutor us to ask God not to lead us into temptation? The answer is found in the meaning of the Greek word. *Peirasmos,* "temptation," can be accurately rendered "tested, tried." We can legitimately ask God not to test us beyond our endurance. It is honest to confess weakness and to appeal for deliverance from our susceptibility to sin.

We smile at Augustine's famous prayer, "Lord, save me from sin, but not yet," but uncomfortably hear ourselves usually not asking for deliverance from our favorite indulgences. Jesus' prayer brings us up short: we are uttering what we would prefer to be left unspoken. We are specifically requesting God's help to prevent us from voluntarily entering into sinful behavior. The evil itself is not the focus, but our participation in it.

Who is "the evil one?" Satan is implied, but sometimes he or she is another person—even a good friend. My old minister used to half-jokingly pray, "Lord, deliver me from my friends. I can take care of my enemies myself." It's not unusual for well-meaning companions to prevent us from being our best selves. They are like Peter trying to dissuade Jesus from persisting on toward Jerusalem and his death. He didn't intend to thwart God's plan. He just wanted to protect his friend. Who hasn't been similarly "rescued" from the will of God?

No part of the Lord's Prayer hits closer to home than this. Don't we all need to be guided away from situations fraught with moral peril? Haven't we all felt the need to have our sagging resistance to evil bolstered? We pray for deliverance from sickness, from fear, from poverty, from unpopularity, but how much more we need deliverance from evil.

The prayer reminds us of who we are. We are the children of a powerful God, members of a powerful support group called the church, responsible persons with others relying on us, and temples of the Holy Spirit of God himself. We have so much already; what more could be gained from consorting with the evil one (or ones) where there is everything to be enjoyed by avoiding him (or them)?

We will not, however, be completely able to avoid evil, not in this world. Paul Tournier's observations are most helpful:

> Faithfulness without temptation to infidelity is not true faithfulness. Faith without temptation or doubt is not true faith. Purity without temptation to impurity is not true purity.[3]

Since we are surrounded, then, by so great a host of temptations, we pray this prayer: Please, Lord, don't give us (or allow us to take on) more than we can handle! ("Lead us not into temptation.") And we mean it. Honestly.

Praise

The doxology was not in the original manuscripts, hence it is usually printed as a footnote in our modern versions.

> For yours is the kingdom
> and the power
> and the glory
> forever.
> Amen.

The words were undoubtedly added to the original model prayer when Christians began reciting it in public worship. The first ending, "Deliver us from evil," was an unsatisfactory conclusion when prayed in unison; something more upbeat was called for. In Jewish services, doxologies were commonly appended to the end of hymns and sometimes at the beginning of prayers. After the resurrection, there was all the more reason for the early Christians to sing a doxology.

When author Katherine Mansfield was in Switzerland, she exulted in the fresh mountain air but, lacking a religious faith, she wrote a friend, "If only one could make some small grasshoppery sound of praise to someone—thanks to someone. But who?" We know the who, and the words of the doxology provide the what.

Hers was the impulse often felt by Abraham Lincoln during his turbulent tenure in the White House. He once confided to the Baltimore Presbyterian Synod, "I was early brought to a living reflection that nothing in my power whatever, in others to rely upon, would succeed without the direct assistance of the Almighty." This spoken by the man who also said, in the same setting, "I have often wished that I was a more devout man than I am." Often feeling inadequate to his overwhelming task, Lincoln further confessed, "Nevertheless, amid the greatest difficulties of my administration, when I could not see any other resort, I would place my whole reliance in God."[4]

We repeat the doxology as testimony to our conviction that on God alone do we rely. The doxology makes explicit what is often left implicit in our prayers and conversation.

I think about God,
Yet I talk of small matters.
Now isn't it odd
How my idle tongue chatters!
Of quarrelsome neighbors,
Fine weather and rain,
Indifferent labors,
Indifferent pain,
Some trivial style
Fashion shifts with a nod.
And yet all the while
I am thinking of God.[5]

Thinking of him leads to thanking him.
So the model prayer (as we have it today) begins and ends with God.

His is the sacred name,
   the perfect will,
      the desirable kingdom
         the dependable power
           and the majesty beyond compare.

And to think he wants to hear from us!

Questions for Discussion

1. The author notes that, except for the Lord's invitation and example, it would be presumptuous for us to dare ask God for favors. What do we communicate to him when we ignore this great invitation?

2. Some people pray wit poetic eloquence. Others use flowery words, but merely give a "performance." What is the difference? How can you tell which is which?
3. How do you keep in balance the personal nature of prayer (to "Our Father") and the concept of approaching the awesome God of the universe?
4. In praying for God's will to be done, what responsibility does the one praying assume? Are you willing to assume such a responsibility?
5. Does praying for daily bread and not worrying about the future suggest Christians ought not to have savings or insurance? Why or why not?
6. Note Jane Merchant's comment about forgiveness on page 28. What *does* Christ expect? How can one meet that expectation?
7. How important is praying for protection from temptation? How can that importance be demonstrated in our prayer lives?
8. How significant is praise in your prayer life? Offer to God a prayer of praise right now!

[1] "The Golden Sayings of Epictetus," XCVII, *The Harvard Classics*, ed. Charles W. Eliot. P.F. Collier and Son Co., 1909. Volume 2, p. 153.

[2] Quoted in *Reader's Digest*, July 1963.

[3] Paul Tournier, *Guilt and Grace*. New York, Evanston: Harper and Row, Publishers, 1958, p. 45.

[4] Elton Trueblood, *Abraham Lincoln, Theologian of American Anguish*. New York, et. al.: Harper and Row, Publishers, 1973, p. 82.

[5] Gamaliel Bradford, quoted in William Stidger, *Planning Your Preaching*. New York and London: Harper and Brothers, Publishers, 1932, p. 219.

Hindrances to Prayer

David Eubanks, President of Johnson Bible College, Knoxville, Tennessee

Prayer is probably the greatest privilege, opportunity, blessing, and responsibility that human beings enjoy. It enables us to communicate personally with the great God of this universe and makes available to us his unlimited power. Stories abound of little known, often obscure, individuals who have wrought wondrous things through prayer, confirming that nothing is impossible with God.

Prayer is universally available to all Christians. Since God is no respecter of persons, prayer is not tied to age, race, wealth, fame, educational status, or geographic location. All Christians stand on equal ground before the Father in prayer, having open access to him through the Son. Every child of God can respond to the invitation of the writer of Hebrews to "approach the throne of grace with confidence, so that we may receive mercy and find grace to help us in our time of need" (Hebrews 4:16).

If prayer is so readily available, so wondrously powerful, and so equally accessible, why is it considered to be the greatest unused power in the universe? Why is it distinguished in its neglect by a large proportion of the church of Jesus Christ? Why do most believers find time to do nearly everything in the world except pray?

The answer to these questions can really be answered in one word: *Satan*. Prayer is Satan's major enemy, and Satan is prayer's greatest foe. Nothing shakes the foundations of Hell more than the prayers of God's people. In C.S. Lewis's Screwtape Letters, the demonic Screwtape admonished his nephew Wormwood to persevere in his efforts to lead people to Hell. Counteracting prayer is the primary strategy that he recommends. "Interfere at any price in any fashion when people start to pray, for real prayer is lethal to our cause." Satan himself could not have said it better.

When Paul commends the armor with which the Christian battles Satan and his forces, the great apostle concludes with a strong call to prayer:

> Pray in the Spirit on all occasions with all kinds of prayers and requests. With this in mind, be alert and always keep on praying for all the saints.
>
> Pray also for me, that whenever I open my mouth, words may be given me so that I will fearlessly make known the mystery of the gospel, for which I am an ambassador in chains. Pray that I may declare it fearlessly, as I should (Ephesians 6:18-20).

In his darkest hour, when our Lord struggled with the temptation to forego the cross, prayer was his primary weapon against Satan. In the same context, He told his closest apostles to "watch and pray so that you will not fall into temptation" (Matthew 26:41). If prayer is vital in overcoming temptation, one of Satan's top priorities, if not the highest, is to obstruct the prayer lives of the saints. If he can stop God's people from praying, his work is unhindered.

When people are inclined to pray, the devil will use every method to render them ineffective. He will create doubts about the real value and efficiency of prayer. He will actually prompt other people, even family and friends, to interfere with praying. He will create drowsiness or plant selfish and diversionary thoughts to frustrate praying. We see him at work in the garden of Gethsemane, prompting the apostles who were closest to Jesus to sleep while our Lord wrestled alone in prayer, even though he had asked them to pray with him during that trying hour.

Ultimately, then, every hindrance to prayer is Satan-inspired. He will oppose it with every device, however simple or complex, that he can use. In the following pages eight of the more obvious and prevalent hindrances to effective prayer will be discussed in the hope that readers will be able to recognize them, understand them, relate to them, and overcome them, persevering in prayer to God.

Lack of Commitment

Polls taken in America in recent years have shown that most members of the church pray (if they pray at all) only minutes (not hours) a week. A thousand and one things occupy our time, but prayer is not one of them. It is a low priority in the religious life of so-called Christian America.

This attitude is not new. Failure to pray has been a human frailty as long as man has been on this planet. Throughout the Old Testament God indicated to his people Israel that he was ready to answer, but they would not pray. James struck directly at this problem early in New Testament times when he said to the believers, "You do not have, because you do not ask God" (James 4:2).

Since Satan is dedicated to preventing, interfering with, or delaying prayer, he is thrilled with the low priority given to it. In fact, he sees that the routine responsibilities of life, compounded by the cares and pleasures of the world, leave little time for prayer, and he provides very plausible excuses to justify this neglect. Believers are encouraged to develop heavy schedules of worthwhile and commendable activities that are designed to advance the kingdom of God, as long as quality prayer time is not one of those activities.

The busier our Lord was, the more he prayed. Although he had no sin to confess, he "often withdrew to lonely places and prayed" (Luke 5:16). Crowds pressed him so intensely that he did not always have time to eat, but he always found time to pray. He prayed all night on many occasions.

It is well known that John Wesley prayed daily for two hours in spite of a travel and preaching schedule that would be taxing even with modern transportation. What may not be as well known is that his wife Susanna spent one to two hours each day in prayer while she was raising nineteen children—feeding them, hand-making all their clothing, and home schooling them with a husband gone much of the time. The secret to the tremendous impact the Wesleys had on their generation was their strong commitment to pray in spite of heavy responsibilities that seemed to leave little time for it.

If the press of our work becomes so great that it squeezes out time for prayer, then the work must be altered. If not, it will be flawed.

> It is better to let the work go by default than to let the praying go by neglect. Whatever affects the intensity of our prayer affects the value of our work. "Too busy to pray" is not only the keynote to backsliding, but it mars even the work done.[1]

Spiritual Laziness

Too many people in our culture want maximum benefits at minimum cost. We live in the age of the "quick fix" and instant gratification. Sometimes it seems that nearly everyone is looking for a shortcut to success and satisfaction.

That same spirit has made its way into the church. Too many Christians want maximum spiritual results without expending more than minimal spiritual energy. Their spiritual activity consists of one or two hours of corporate worship (one hour preferable) each week, little or no serious Bible study, less than even a little in financial stewardship, and little or no serious personal effort to evangelize the lost. Is it any wonder that prayer is relegated to a brief devotional, if even that, at the beginning or end of the day?

Prayer that changes lives, alters homes, moves churches, affects our culture, and wins the lost is more than that. It is hard work. E. M. Bounds wrote,

> Prayer is not a little habit pinned on us while we were tied to our mother's apron strings; neither is it a little decent quarter of a minute's grace said over an hour's dinner, but it is a most serious work of our most serious years. . . . Spiritual work is taxing work, and men are loath to do it. Praying, true praying, costs an outlay of serious attention and of time, which flesh and blood do not relish.[2]

A successful and powerful prayer life often develops out of struggle. Some of the greatest prayer warriors in the history of the church have been people who won their prayer stripes through conflict. The apostle Paul shouldered responsibilities and cares, kept up a fast pace of activities, and endured waves of persecution that almost defy our sense of reality. Accordingly, his letters testify to an intensive and exhaustive prayer life. For example, he exhorted the Romans: "I urge you, brothers, by our Lord Jesus Christ and by the love of the Spirit, to join me in my struggle by praying to God for me" (Romans 15:30). David Brainerd prayed once "in such anguish, and pleaded with so much earnestness and importunity" that he felt "extremely weak and overcome. . . . I could scarcely walk straight . . . my joints were loosed, the sweat ran down my face and body, and nature seemed as if it would dissolve."[3]

Luke captures the toilsome nature of our Lord's Gethsemane prayer experience graphically: "And being in anguish, he prayed more earnestly, and his sweat was like drops of blood falling to the ground" (Luke 22:44). The writer of Hebrews summarizes many such experiences when he writes, "During the days of Jesus' life on earth, he offered up prayers and petitions with loud cries and tears" (Hebrews 5:7). No one will learn from Jesus that prayer is an easy road.

The Word of God abounds with illustrations of victories won through toilsome prayer. Nehemiah's rebuilding of the walls of Jerusalem against tremendous odds was punctuated by prayer and preceded by three months of fasting and praying before "the God of heaven" (Nehemiah 1:4; 2:4). Only then was the project presented to King Artaxerxes, whose help was vitally needed. Daniel's perseverance in prayer is legendary. On one occasion, he prayed for twenty-one days for revelation from God. The angel of the Lord who was delivering it was delayed by the forces of evil for twenty-one days. With powerful help from Michael, however, he brought the answer to Daniel's prayer on the twenty-first day (Daniel 10).

The Bible not only provides positive examples but shows us how to overcome neglect and laziness in prayer. James says, "Resist the devil, and he will flee from you" (James 4:7). Like Daniel, we must establish regular times for prayer and keep on praying. Jesus says, "Ask and it will be given to you" (Matthew 7:7). So let us ask for help in making prayer a high priority, overcoming the distractions of Satan and concentrating on the Lord.

Praying Selfishly

James captures this errant spirit of prayer in a nutshell: "When you ask, you do not receive, because you ask with wrong motives, that you may spend what you get on your pleasures" (James 4:3). Prayer is not looking upon God as the great Santa Claus in the sky who will give us everything on our wish list.

Does James mean that there is no place in prayer to ask for anything for oneself? Some people think so. They believe only praise to God or asking in behalf of others is appropriate for prayer. To pray for oneself is wrong, they say.

Jesus surely taught otherwise. He told his disciples to pray for each day's bread, to be forgiven of their trespasses, and not to be led into temptation. To pray for oneself is not to pray selfishly. Our Lord knows his people have needs; he expects, indeed, commands that they pray for those needs to be met.

Selfish praying is motivated by gratification of our sensual desires in contrast to seeking the will and glorification of God. Greed is a prime example. Most people seem to have a natural desire to want more and more of the things of this world and never to be satisfied with what they have. Prayer is often invoked to gratify this desire. God will not answer that prayer. One of the most extreme examples of such praying on record is that of John Ward, past member of the British Parliament:

> O Lord, thou knowest that I have nine houses in the city of London, and that I have lately purchased an estate in Essex. I beseech Thee to preserve the two counties of Middlesex and Essex from fire and earthquakes. And as I have also a mortgage in Hertfordshire, I beg thee also to have an eye of compassion on that county, and for the rest of the counties, Thou mayest deal with them as Thou mayest. O Lord, enable the banks to answer all their bills, and make all the debtors good men. Give prosperous voyage and safe return to the Mermaid Sloop, because I have not insured it. And because Thou hath said, 'The days of the wicked are but short,' I trust Thee that Thou wilt not forget Thy promise, as I have an estate that I will inherit on the death of that poor profligate young man, Sir. J. L. Preserve me from thieves and housebreakers, and make all my servants so honest and faithful that they may always attend to my interests, and never cheat me out of my property night or day.[4]

Selfish praying is prayer that is too concerned with self, perhaps even for seemingly legitimate reasons, and not enough with Christ. The goal of our lives and our prayers should be to glorify the Lord and to see his authority and kingdom spread over all the earth. He himself captured this spirit in John 14:13: "And I will do whatever you ask in my name, so that the Son may bring glory to the Father." The same attitude dominated Paul's life and prayers. His words to the church at Thessalonica provide one example:

> Finally, brothers, pray for us that the message of the Lord may spread rapidly and be honored, just as it was with you. And pray that we may be delivered from wicked and evil men, for not everyone has faith. . . . May the Lord direct your hearts into God's love and Christ's perseverance (2 Thessalonians 3:1, 2, 5).

What a contrast between the prayer of John Ward and the prayers of Paul!

Sin

After a tremendous victory at Jericho, Israel was stopped in its tracks during the invasion of Canaan because, as God told Joshua, "Israel has sinned" (Joshua 7:11). Until the sin was rooted out, there was no hope of going forward.

Unrepented sin totally frustrates prayer. Psychologically, no conscientious person who has any sense of the holiness of God can approach him in an unrepentant state. As Shakespeare's Claudius, who was living in open incest with the wife of the brother whom he had murdered, said concerning his efforts to pray,

> My words fly up, my thoughts remain below.
> Words without thoughts never to heaven go
> (*Hamlet*, III, Sc. 2, line 97)

David, man after God's own heart, declared, "If I had cherished sin in my heart, the Lord would not have listened"

(Psalm 66:18). Our own minds rebel against the thought of praying to God while we continue to sin against him.

More importantly, God has made clear that he will not respond to the unrepentant sinner. Isaiah prophesied to the sinful Israelites,

> But your iniquities have separated you from your God;
> your sins have hidden his face from you,
> so that he will not hear (Isaiah 59:2).

Later the elders of Israel in Babylon came to Ezekiel for prayer in their behalf, the very kind of response that he had sought so earnestly from them in spiritual matters. But the word of the Lord came to him: "Son of man, these men have set up idols in their hearts and put wicked stumbling blocks before their faces. Should I let them inquire of me at all?" (Ezekiel 14:3). God would not listen. While we have idols in our hearts, he will not hear.

It is not the fact that we have sinned that obstructs our prayers. All have sinned and come short of the glory of God. Unrepented, unconfessed sin is the problem. "If we confess our sins, he is faithful and just and will forgive us our sins and purify us from all unrighteousness" (1 John 1:9). James says, "Confess your sins to each other and pray for each other that you may be healed. The prayer of a righteous man is powerful and effective" (James 5:16).

Isaiah was ready to be used mightily by God after he had seen the Lord in all his glory and holiness and confessed, "Woe to me! . . . I am ruined! For I am a man of unclean lips, and I live among a people of unclean lips" (Isaiah 6:5). When Ezra realized fully the sins of Israel, he tore his garments, pulled out some of his hair, and went to the Lord in fasting and prayer, confessing, "O my God, I am too ashamed and disgraced to lift up my face to you, my God, because our sins are higher than our heads and our guilt has reached to the heavens" (Ezra 9:6). After Daniel clearly understood the visions of God that came to him concerning the desolation of Jerusalem for seventy years, he "turned to the Lord God and pleaded with him in prayer and petition, in fasting, and in sackcloth and ashes. I prayed to the Lord my God and confessed . . ." (Daniel 9:3, 4). There followed one of the most marvelous prayers of confession on behalf of a nation that ever came from human lips. One of the greatest men of prayer who ever lived, Paul, acknowledged, "Here is a trustworthy saying that deserves full acceptance: Christ Jesus came into the world to save sinners—of whom I am the worst" (1 Timothy 1:15).

It may seem paradoxical to some that, although sin separates us from God and is the major hindrance to effective prayer, many of the greatest prayer warriors have been people with a keen sense of their own sins who excelled in repentance and confession in prayer. Moreover, prayer is our primary help in gaining forgiveness and overcoming the grip of sin. It was the publican, prayerfully beating his breast and confessing, "God, have mercy on me, a sinner," who went home justified rather than the Pharisee who vainly praised his own virtues to the Lord (Luke 18:10-14).

When sin has been confessed and the heart is purified before God, we can approach him with boldness. All obstructions to sincere and powerful petition are removed. As John writes, "If our hearts do not condemn us, we have confidence before God and receive from him anything we ask, because we obey his commands and do what pleases him" (1 John 3:21).

Neglect of God's Word

One can study the Bible without praying, but no one can be successful in prayer apart from the Word, which is the foundation of all prayer. Where else can we learn about God and his nature and power, and about prayer and how we relate to him through it? One of history's greatest prayer warriors was George Mueller. Mr. Mueller fed thousands of orphans in England by depending entirely on faith in God through prayer. On one occasion, Mueller was asked how many times he had read the Bible. He replied, "I have read it through sixty-six times, and I am now going through it for the sixty-seventh time, and it gets more interesting and sweeter every time I read it." Surely there was a connection between Mueller's effectiveness in prayer and his study of the Word.

For one thing, God will not hear the prayers of a person who ignores his Word. "If anyone turns a deaf ear to the law, even his prayers are detestable" (Proverbs 28:9). On the other hand, David fills his psalms with declarations of his love, respect, and admiration for God's Word; his statutes, laws, and precepts. His psalms, for the most part, are beautiful prayer songs to God.

If we stay away from God's Word, we miss the most significant preparation for prayer. Some of the most beautiful, powerful, and persuasive prayers ever prayed are recorded in the Bible: Moses' prayers in behalf of Israel, David's prayers in the Psalms, Solomon's prayer at the dedication of the temple, Nehemiah's prayers before and during the rebuilding of the wall of Jerusalem, Daniel's marvelous prayer on behalf of Israel in Daniel 9, Jesus' prayers, especially those in John 17 and in the garden of Gethsemane. From these and others we learn how to pray. In fact, apart from the Bible, how can we develop the concepts and language of prayer?

Sincere study of the Word also prepares one's spirit to enter into the presence of God. Charles Spurgeon preached,

> In times of peril and distress we may even fly to God just as we are, as the dove enters the cleft of the rock, even though her plumes are ruffled; but in ordinary times we should not come with an unprepared spirit; even as a child comes not to his father in the morning until he has washed his face.[5]

Mueller confessed that often he could not pray until he had "steadied" his mind on a text. There can be no better preparation for prayer than quiet meditation on the Word of the one to whom we pray.

Lack of Faith

Since doubt is one of Satan's deadliest weapons, prayer is often hindered by lack of faith. Through the trials and hardships of life, people are tempted to doubt that God answers prayer. Sometimes, even though they believe that God answers prayer in general, they may be tempted to doubt that he will answer their prayers in particular or doubt that he will answer prayer for a specific cause. In any case, just as it is impossible to please God without faith, so it is impossible to pray effectively to him without faith.

Jesus promised, "If you believe, you will receive whatsoever you ask for in prayer," and included "do not doubt" as a condition of faith for prayer to be answered (Matthew 21:21, 22). James says that anyone who asks of God "must believe and not doubt, because he who doubts is like a wave of the sea, blown and tossed by the wind. That man should not think he will receive anything from the Lord" (James 1:6, 7). He also affirms that "the prayer offered in faith will make the sick person well" (James 5:15).

Praying in faith is more than mere lack of doubt. It is the absolute confidence that God is over all and nothing is impossible with him. It is also submitting to the ultimate will of the Father as Jesus did in the garden of Gethsemane. Surely it is the assurance that "in all things God works for the good of those who love him, who have been called according to his purpose" (Romans 8:28).

If we are convinced that our prayers are being hindered by lack of faith, what can we do? Ironic as it may seem, we can pray for increased faith to pray more effectively. The apostles did. They said to the Lord, "Increase our faith!" (Luke 17:5). Jesus said to the father of the boy with the evil spirit who pleaded with him to heal his son, "Everything is possible for him who believes." The man replied, "I do believe; help me overcome my unbelief!" (Mark 9:23, 24). What more appropriate prayer could we pray?

In Romans 12:3 Paul refers to the "measure of faith" that God gives to believers. Referring to earthly fathers who give good gifts to some who ask them, Jesus said that our Father in Heaven will "give the Holy Spirit to those who ask him" (Luke 11:11-13). We may not understand all that these two Scriptures mean, but they surely indicate that God will enlarge and strengthen the faith of any of his children who sincerely pray for increased faith.

Lack of Persistence

Our prayers are often ineffective because we give up too soon. In Luke 18 Jesus told the parable of a widow who asked a judge to avenge her of her adversary. At first the judge disregarded her, but because she persisted, troubling and bothering him by her continual requests, he finally gave her justice. Luke simply says that Jesus told this story to the people "to show them that they should always pray and not give up" (Luke 18:1).

God is unlike the judge of Jesus' parable in that he is just and he is eager to respond to our prayers. Still, in his infinite wisdom he has determined persistence as an essential ingredient of a complete prayer life. While he does on occasion answer a request immediately, many of his answers come only after days, months, years, even decades of persistent prayer. Someone has said, "prayer is digging holes, planting poles, and hanging wire."

Paul challenges us with a victorious prayer strategy in Ephesians 6:18: "Pray in the Spirit on all occasions with all kinds of prayers and requests. With this in mind, be alert and always keep on praying for all the saints." Anyone who sincerely and consistently maintains this attitude of persistence in prayer will be rewarded. When God was about to destroy the nation of Israel after they had turned away from him, and Israel's very existence hung in the balance, Moses passionately and exhaustively prayed on their behalf for forty days and nights. Finally God relented and mercifully spared them. Moses had saved a nation by persistent prayer. Because Daniel persevered in prayer for nearly seventy years in behalf of Israel, God blessed his life daily and his people benefitted wonderfully in the end. A seven-day prayer meeting preceded Pentecost as the apostles and disciples "all joined together constantly in prayer" (Acts 1:14).

Perhaps one serendipitous value of persistence in prayer is that we find our own attitudes and lives changing for the better. When Jacob wrestled with God at Peniel he was intent on receiving a blessing and asking God's name, but he left in humility and reverence saying, "I saw God face to face" (Genesis 32:24-30).

An Unforgiving Spirit

An unforgiving spirit interferes with prayer in two ways. First, it interferes with the sincere, open heart necessary for spiritual contact with God. Nothing is more self-destructive than a critical, condemning, and implacable attitude. How can we communicate with a merciful and forgiving God if we hold malice, ill will, and resentment in our hearts toward others? Psychologically our minds will not permit that communication, even when we are convinced of the rightness of our position.

In the second place, God has made clear that he will not forgive those who refuse to forgive. Jesus said, "And when you stand praying, if you hold anything against anyone, forgive him, so that your Father in heaven may forgive you your sins" (Mark 11:25). He taught his disciples to pray, "Forgive us our debts, as we also have forgiven our debtors" (Matthew 6:12). He told the parable of the unmerciful servant in Matthew 18 to contrast the enormity of God's forgiveness toward us with the smallness of our forgiveness of each other, and underscored that God's magnanimous mercy toward us will be forfeited by our refusal to extend mercy to others. Prayer and forgiveness are inseparable: God's forgiveness of us and our forgiveness of each other.

God has done everything to make prayer freely available to his people, but Satan, fearful of its power, continues to place obstacles in our way. Finding ways to reduce our commitment and to make us lazy, selfish, sinful, and negligent of God's Word; weakening our faith, diminishing our persistence, hardening our hearts to the repentance of others—these are a few of the strategies of Satan to rob us of the privilege, opportunity, and blessing of prayer. But we are not without resources to fight back.

Indeed, our greatest strategy may be an open confession of our condition and a genuine prayer for God's help. History's greatest prayer warriors have from time to time experienced disappointment with their prayer lives. In his wonderful little book, *The Meaning of Prayer*, Fosdick quotes the following from the diary of Benjamin Jowett:

> Nothing makes one more conscious of poverty and shallowness of character than difficulty in praying or attending to prayer. Any thoughts about self, thoughts of evil, day dreams, love fancies, easily find an abode in the mind. But the thought of God and of right and truth will not stay there, except with a very few persons. I fail to understand my own nature in this particular. There is nothing at a distance I seem to desire more than the knowledge of God, the ideal, the universal; and yet for two minutes I cannot keep my mind upon them. But I read a great work of fiction, and can hardly take my mind from it. If I had any real love of God, would not my mind dwell upon him? [6]

Fosdick follows this confession with a prayer by Samuel McComb. When our own prayers fail us, we might do well to learn from the prayers of others. In the original prayer McComb seems to speak of himself in the third person. While maintaining the archaic language of this old prayer, I have rewritten it in first person. I close this chapter by inviting you to read it and, if necessary, pray it again and again as your prayer. It will help you overcome the obstacles.

Gracious Father, who gives the hunger of desire, and satisfies our hunger with good things; quicken the heart of Your servant who mourns because I cannot speak to You, nor hear You speak to me. Refresh, I beseech Thee, the dullness and dryness of my inner life. Grant me perseverance that I may never abandon the effort to pray, even if it brings for a time no comfort or joy. Enlarge my soul's desires that I may be drawn unto You. Send forth Your Spirit into my heart to help my infirmities; to give me freedom of utterance, and warmth of feeling. Let me muse upon Your goodness; upon the blessings with which You have strewn my path; upon the mystery of the world, and the shame of sin, and the sadness of death—until the fire kindles and the heart melts in prayer and praise and supplication.

Lord, teach me to pray the prayer that relieves the burdened spirit, and brings Your blessing, which makes us rich and adds no sorrow. Hear us, for Jesus' sake. Amen.[7]

Questions for Discussion

1. The author describes prayer as "the greatest privilege, opportunity, blessing, and responsibility that human beings enjoy." Do you agree or disagree? Why?
2. If prayer is such a great asset to the Christian, why do you think it is so sadly neglected?
3. The author lists the following hindrances to prayer. Which is the most troubling to you? What can you do to defeat this hindrance?

Lack of commitment	Spiritual laziness
Praying selfishly	Sin
Neglect of God's Word	Lack of faith
Lack of persistence	An unforgiving spirit

4. Of the hindrances the author lists (see #3), which do you think is most troubling to your church as a whole? What can the church do corporately to overcome these hindrances? Suggest one idea to combat each hindrance.

5. The author says, "Some of the greatest prayer warriors in the history of the church have . . . won their prayer stripes through conflict." Has conflict helped you improve your prayer life? If so, how? What was the nature of the conflict?

6. Clearly, praying only for one's own needs is selfish. The author observes, however, that it is appropriate to include one's own needs in prayer. How much praying for one's own needs is appropriate? Is it 50 percent? Twenty-five? Ten? What guidelines would you suggest to keep from becoming selfish in prayer?

7. Would you add any other hindrances to the author's list?

8. Why do you think the author did not suggest "lack of time" as a hindrance to prayer?

9. If, as the author states, Satan is behind every hindrance to prayer, what should be the Christian's attitude toward any obstruction to his or her prayer time? How can you keep this attitude in mind when you are busy and find your prayer time being crowded out?

---

[1] E. M. Bounds, *The Weapon of Prayer.* Grand Rapids: Baker, 1975, p. 13.

[2] Dick Eastman, *No Easy Road: Inspirational Thoughts on Prayer.* Grand Rapids: Baker, 1971, p. 12.

[3] D.M. McIntyre, *The Hidden Life of Prayer.* Grand Rapids: Baker, 1979, p. 21.

[4] Leonard Ravenhill, *Why Revival Tarries.* Minneapolis: Bethany Fellowship, Inc., 1959, p. 158.

[5] Charles Spurgeon, *Twelve Sermons on Prayer.* Grand Rapids: Baker, 1971, p. 34.

[6] Harry E. Fosdick, *The Meaning of Prayer.* New York: Association Press, 1915, p. 74.

[7] Ibid.

Pray for Revival

Robert F. Yawberg, Senior Minister of Broadway Christian Church, Ft. Wayne, IN; Founder of Prayer-a-Gram Ministries

I have never been able to forget one elder's prayer. He stood by the Communion table and said, "Lord, help us to think back to when your Son was still living. . . ."

Jesus not alive now? Only a memory? Lord only of the past?

Jesus is alive! It is the church that is lacking life. How do we bring new life to the body of Christ in this age?

I believe the burning need of the church today is genuine Holy Spirit revival. Nothing less than the return of Christ's life, vital and power-filling, will suffice. Such revival begins with prayer, personal and corporate.

I am not referring to the traditional one-week evangelistic meeting held every year. Nor do I mean raw emotion that produces mere shouting or a few more crocodile tears. The church desperately needs the reviving of Jesus' life, the return of his Holy Spirit's power and purity.

Thirty years ago a preacher told me of a movement of people restoring the church to its first-century doctrine and practice. What he read to me from the book of Acts was fascinating and new. The denomination I was in then had lost such vision. As he read God's Word to me, the vision in my heart was rekindled.

I joined with thousands of other New Testament believers in an attempt to revive a dying body. At times there would be signs of life. During our annual "revival meeting" everyone would redouble his efforts, and for a few weeks much progress was made. But before long our peak effort ceased, and again the life would ebb away, and the old law came back to haunt us. We just couldn't do enough on a sustained basis to keep the engines running and the wheels turning.

After years of work, I have been led to a much different approach. It is not enough for me to try harder in the ongoing effort to restore life to the church. Only God through his Holy Spirit can do that! Only God through his Spirit-breathed Word can energize a weary and worn people whose muscles are aching and feet are dragging.

Do you not know? Have you not heard?
The Everlasting God, the Lord, the Creator of the ends of the
    earth
Does not become weary or tired. . . .
He gives strength to the weary,
And to him who lacks might he increases power
                                          (Isaiah 40:28, 29).

When I look back over periods of church history, I see how God and God alone gave life to his church.

Pray for Revival

What then are we to do? Prayer is the place to begin! It has been so from the time of our Lord's physical presence.

Jesus prayed! Jesus prayed at his baptism and the Holy Spirit came upon him. He prayed when hard pressed. He prayed when people misunderstood him and left him alone. He spent the night in prayer before selecting the twelve men in whom he would invest his life. He prayed and was transfigured. He prayed and Lazarus emerged from the grave, alive! He prayed in the garden when all had deserted him. From the cross, Jesus prayed for his enemies, "Father, forgive them; for they do not know what they are doing" (Luke 23:34). He called his men to pray. They responded by pleading, "Lord, teach us to pray."

Jesus' words come to me again today: "So, you men could not keep watch with me for one hour? Keep watching and praying, that you may not enter into temptation; the spirit is willing, but the flesh is weak" (Matthew 26:40-41).

I was invited to speak to a group of fellow preachers on the theme, "The Minister's Personal Prayer Life." Facing those twenty men, what could I say that had not already been said? They knew how to pray. And yet I sensed that not a single man there that morning was satisfied with his prayer life.

PRAYERLESSNESS! The symptom of our restless pilgrimage for growth and prosperity in the church and our personal careers is prayerlessness. I confessed to these brothers my own prayerlessness. The confession struck a responsive chord. After a study of John 17 (Jesus' prayer for himself, his men, and his church today) we went off by twos and prayed. Not only did we pray there, but upon leaving, we promised to pray for one another over the next thirty days.

The need of the hour is to pray. Pray for God's life to invade his church again.

The basic difference between Christians of the first century and those of this century is that they prayed while we talk about prayer. They prayed and the building shook, the Holy Spirit possessed them, and they spoke the name of Jesus in boldness! We talk about prayer, but a host of barriers arise and we just don't get to it. There will be no lasting revival in the church until we not only believe in prayer, but believe enough to pray.

It is unfortunate when people fail to communicate with one another, but it is tragic when people fail to communicate with God. The prophets cared more about what God thought than what men thought. This keen perception of being God's person comes only after much praying. Praying is like talking with a friend. True prayer breaks down the barriers and opens the heart.

What do you do when you don't feel like praying? Pray until you do feel like it. Prayer must come out of obedience, not emotion. Jesus' prayer life is a model for all ages. If our Lord needed to pray, how much more do we!

When people most sought Christ, he most sought God. "In the early morning, while it was still dark, he arose and went out and departed to a lonely place, and was praying there. . . . And they found him, and said to him, 'Everyone is looking for you'" (Mark 1:35, 37).

Several times in my life and ministry, prayer has made the difference between giving up or going on. When my wife, Marilyn, and I were being called to leave our first ministry, we prayed. We had no desire to leave our home and church family, but the church in suburban Fort Wayne, Indiana, was persistent. We prayed together again and again, pleading with the Lord for an answer. Several days later, a preacher friend confronted me. "Bob," he said, "you need to change ministries. You have been in Neapolis long enough!" Upon my arrival home that evening, I found Marilyn had also received direction for leaving. It came as she stood praying at her ironing board that same afternoon. God had heard and answered our prayers.

A year later in my first suburban ministry I heard a man speak who changed my prayer life. Dr. Harold Ockenga, then pastor of Park Street Church in Boston, was lecturing on preaching at nearby Huntington College. "Before you can learn to preach," he reminded us, "you must know how to pray!" He then told us how to begin a prayer list. I went home that day and began a discipline that continues even now. It meant writing on paper the simple statement, "Lord, I can't handle all these heartaches and problems people continue to bring to me. I can't even handle my own very well. In writing them here, I release them to you and will no longer carry them" (cf. Matthew 11:28-30).

I added blank sheets to the notebook. Each time another need arose, I recorded it with the date and space for more notations. Soon the list had grown to hundreds of requests. Amazed over how many God answered, I began marking them with a red pen—ANSWERED—boldly across the petition. God had been answering many more of my prayers than I realized. Often I had forgotten I had even asked.

The first request ever written on that list took six years before an answer came. Golden Years Homestead, a Christian home for the aged, was only a dream in 1965. Through persistent prayer and hard work by many, the home became a reality in 1971.

I like what LeRoy Trulock once said: "My greatest delight is helping God answer my prayer." Mr. Trulock believed in prayer, but he also believed in action that enables God to use his life as part of the answer. It is not enough just to pray and then do nothing. The world has turned its back on many "pious people" who talk all the time about prayer but never get any results.

Our church broke ground for a long-awaited building program in 1973. Days later, we learned the promised bank loan was not available. We were driven to prayer. Having heard of the early morning prayer meetings in Korea, I announced on a Sunday morning, "We will meet at 5:30 A.M. for prayer tomorrow and continue daily until we find the Lord's answer to our dilemma."

Little did we know it would require over forty consecutive days of such prayer discipline before we gained direction. The answer came unexpectedly as eighty families from our congregation were led to establish a new work in the central city of Fort Wayne. My family went with the new work. The mother church later completed the long awaited building. Without daily prayer over a sustained period of time, we would have missed God's open door.

This prayer taken from my journal records the uncertainty and need of that hour:

> O God, the years have passed—you are still here. Thank you for seeing me through these six weeks. On this Wednesday morning I am weary and somewhat confused. you have called me to a new ministry. But I need time with you! Why have you called *me*? Days and days of rumor, falsehood and pressure have been overcome through you, dear Jesus. Now I stand on the threshold of a new experience and I am not capable of any way to handle it—apart from you, my Lord and my God. Hear me now and lead me. In Christ, Amen.

For eight years I met early every Wednesday morning with a few fellow pastors who became real brothers in prayer. We came from different denominational backgrounds, yet shared a common hunger and desire to bear one another's burdens. It was out of those early mornings with the Lord that the Citizens for Decency Through Law movement in Fort Wayne began in 1982, resulting in the closing of three hard core porn stores 2 1/2 years later.

Now on Sunday mornings when we leave home, Marilyn and I stand hand in hand as she prays for my day. She prays for me to be the man God has called me to be. I pray often for her, sometimes over the phone when she's facing a difficult decision or counseling situation. Our prayer times together have helped build a strong relationship in our marriage, now in its thirty-eighth year.

Above all, prayer is practicing the presence of Jesus. It is not merely a set hour. It may not be on our knees or even with eyes closed. To pray without ceasing should be our goal! To awaken with "Lord, good morning. I invite you to control my life today." And moment by moment to speak often and listen much as the Spirit of Jesus dwells in us. Brother Lawrence in *The Practice of the Presence of God* says it well. "The time of business does not differ with me from the time of prayer; and, in the noise and clatter of my kitchen I possess God in as great tranquility as if I were on my knees at the blessed sacrament."

Early in our present ministry, I made a decision about the midweek meeting. Rather than assemble with the "faithful few" at the building each week, Marilyn and I invited a few people to our home. We selected those recently baptized and others who had inquired about the church. For the past fifteen years, we have continued to meet with groups of ten or twelve for a period of six weeks. I teach them biblical truths on what it means to seriously follow Jesus. I pray with the men and Marilyn prays with the women as we close each session. There, with a few new-found friends, needs are confessed and prayers spoken. Praying together specifically for one another has made a profound effect on this congregation.

Remember one thing—wherever Christ is, anything can happen. And he is here!

Bakht Singh, a Christian leader in India writes,

The indigenous churches in India have a great burden for America just now . . . and are praying that God will visit your country with revival. . . . You feel sorry for us in India because of our poverty in material things. We who know the Lord in India feel sorry for you in America because of your spiritual poverty. We pray that God may give you gold tried in the fire, which He has promised to those who know the power of His resurrection. . . . In our churches we spend four to five or six hours in prayer and worship, and frequently our people wait on the Lord in prayer all night; but in America after one hour, you begin to look at your watches. We pray that God may open your eyes to the true meaning of worship. To attract people to meetings, you have a great dependence on posters, on advertising, on promotion, and on the buildup of the human being; in India we have nothing more than the Lord himself and we find that He is sufficient. Before a Christian meeting in India we never announce who the speaker will be. When the people come, they come to seek the Lord and not a human being or to hear some special favorite speaking to them. We have had as many as 12,000 people come together just to worship the Lord and to have fellowship together. We are praying that the people in America might also come to church with a hunger for God and not merely a hunger to see some form of amusement or hear choirs or the voice of any man.

Richard Owen Roberts reminds us that "revival is the work of God." He continues:

No amount of human effort can produce true revival. There is much that people can do, and all that we can do we should do—with all our might. Men can and must evangelize; it is part of the Great Commission. Men can and must train Christian workers if we are to honor our Lord's command. We can teach new converts the way of Christ and baptize them in the name of the Father, Son, and Holy Spirit. This, too, is part of the Great Commission. We can pray; this burden is placed upon every believer. We must concern ourselves with the social needs of the world to be true to the call of God to his church. Everything God has told us to do we ought to do, but having done it all, we must still wait upon Him to do what He alone can do. Revival comes from God.[1]

Revive Thy work, O Lord!
Thy mighty arm make bare;
Speak with the voice that wakes the dead,
And make Thy people hear.

Revive Thy work, O Lord!
Create soul-thirst for Thee;
But hung'ring for the bread of life,
Oh, may our spirits be!

Revive! revive!
And give refreshing show'rs;
The glory shall be all Thine own;
The blessing shall be ours.[2]

Questions for Discussion

1. Why do the efforts generated by "evangelistic meetings" seem to wane after just a few short weeks? What is the difference between the kind of hype that expires quickly and the power that drives us on indefinitely?

2. How are the attempts to follow the New Testament pattern for the life of the church and dependence on the power of the Spirit complementary? Can either exist without the other? Why or why not?

3. How often does anyone pray for revival in your church? In your home? Why?

4. The author cites LeRoy Trulock, who refers to "helping God answer my prayer." Do you agree that one can help God answer prayer, or is prayer rightly left to things only God alone can do? Support your answer with Scripture.

5. At what point do our efforts to help God answer our prayers become attempts to answer our own prayers without God's help? What is the proper balance between doing nothing and trying to do it all?

6. Read the words of Bakht Singh (pages 57, 58).How do you think most American Christians would respond if God answered the prayer of "gold tried by fire"? How would you respond?

7. Why do you think Christians in some countries will turn out in huge numbers for lengthy worship services and American Christians will not? Is it simply a matter of devotion, or are there other factors? Would you attend a church whose worship services took three or four hours? Why or why not?

8. Describe what you think your church would be like if God sent true revival. Pray for that result.

---

[1]Richard Owen Roberts, *Revival.* Tyndale House Publishers, Inc., 1982, p. 22.

[2]Alfred Midlane and James McGranahan, "Revive Thy Work." From *Favorite Hymns of Praise*, Tabernacle Pub. Co., Chicago, 1967.

Prayer as Intimacy With God

David Butts, Senior Minister of the Kansas Christian Church, Kansas, IL; Prayer Chairman of a national task force on missions

Most churches are busy churches. We have youth programs and senior citizen programs along with music and ladies' programs. Programs come from busy committees like the missions, evangelism, building, and . . . well, the list could go on and on. There's certainly nothing wrong with programs and committees, as long as they don't distract from what is really essential in the Christian life.

We are often in danger of choosing the important over the essential. Christian service is important. Serving on committees and developing programs that help the church carry out its mission is vital. But we tend to be so activity-oriented we often forget that the heart of Christianity is a relationship with a person, the person of Jesus Christ. This essential relationship often takes a backseat to our Christian service.

In our prayer lives we often overlook this personal relationship with the Lord. We come to God with our lists. We pray for the sick, the missionaries, our country, the church, our families, our finances—and the list continues. And properly so. We ought to be praying for all of these individuals and situations on a daily basis. But too often that is where our prayers end. What happened to relationship? Where in our prayers have we drawn near to God?

Restoring this missing element in our prayer lives will rejuvenate us spiritually and enable us to carry on in their service to the Lord. There is a lot of discussion today about burnout in the church. Among those who serve and care and give of themselves, there seems to be a point of breakdown. An exhaustion, physically and emotionally as well as spiritually, saps them of their strength to continue service. I believe that many of the problems relating to burnout can be overcome by a restoration of relationship in prayer. It is what we might call intimacy with God in prayer.

We are not the only ones who desire an intimate relationship. From Genesis to Revelation we read of a God who loves his people and desires to have fellowship with them. At least one of the reasons God created people was to have fellowship, to enjoy times spent together. We can only imagine what it was like for Adam and Eve to share such close fellowship with God as he walked with them in the cool of the garden. But we can know more than we do, as we spend time with our Father, growing in intimacy and fellowship.

After they sinned and were expelled from the garden of Eden, that fellowship was severed. The rest of Scripture shows that God was willing to allow his own Son to die on a Roman cross. Intimacy with God has its origin in the mind of God rather than in our desires.

Since this is such an important matter to God, it also needs to be high on our list of priorities. As we commit ourselves to grow in intimacy with God through prayer, it is important that we examine biblical accounts of those who had this intimate walk with God. It will help us better grasp how special a close relationship can be.

The One Thing That's Needed

David provides one of the best examples of intimacy with God in prayer. David was also a fine example of a sinner—an adulterer and murderer, with a list of family problems that doesn't quit. David, a man after God's own heart? How could that be?

In spite of his sins and problems, David longed for intimacy with God. Feel David's passion in this psalm:

> O God, you are my God,
>> earnestly I seek you;
> my soul thirsts for you,
>> my body longs for you,
> in a dry and weary land
>> where there is no water.
> I have seen you in the sanctuary
>> and beheld your power and your glory.
> Because your love is better than life,
>> my lips will glorify you.
> I will praise you as long as I live,
>> and in your name I will lift up my hands.
> My soul will be satisfied as with the richest of foods;
>> with singing lips my mouth will praise you.
> On my bed I remember you;
>> I think of you through the watches of the night.
> Because you are my help,
>> I sing in the shadow of your wings.
> I stay close to you;
>> your right hand upholds me (Psalm 63:1-8).

Let's look closer at this psalm to see how we might draw near to God as David did.

An Expression of Desire

The psalmist cries out for God, expressing his desire for intimacy with him. Could it be that we are not intimate with God because we don't want to be? Have we never got thirsty enough to desire him and him alone? Are our lives so saturated with things and activities that we have never really missed being alone with God? Perhaps our prayer needs to be, "God, create a longing within me for you. Make me thirsty for the living water that is in you."

Remembrance of God's Glory

David refers back to times of worship when he had experienced God's presence in a very special way. He remembers this with joy and longs for more such experiences. So should we. Yet often we fear the emotional response that occurs when we encounter God in times of intense worship. As we pray and worship, we may experience joy, weeping, exhilaration, fear, or other emotions. Rather than dealing with our emotions, we often do the unthinkable—we avoid encounter with God. So we find ourselves with a generation of Christians with no passion toward God, fearful of their own emotional response should they actually encounter the God of the universe.

This attitude is not biblical Christianity. Psalm 63 is the emotional, passionate prayer of a man who had experienced intimacy with God and desired more of the same.

Expressions of Praise

The prayer of intimacy is a prayer of praise. The more we get to know God, the more we will desire to praise him. The exciting thing about our great and wonderful God is that we can never plumb the depths of his nature. There is always something new and exciting about his love, grace, or holiness that will bring forth praise from the lips of the worshiper.

The praise spoken of here is private, personal worship; an intimate time of praise by an individual for his creator. How much more meaningful our Sunday morning corporate worship would be if it were the culmination of a week of personal praise by the individual members of the body of Christ!

We need to teach more about how to worship, especially in our private times alone with God. Many good resources of taped worship music are available today. These can be a great help for personal worship times.

Spontaneous Times With God

Having a planned time for devotions each day is the beginning place for intimacy with God, not the whole matter. Intimacy with God is not only planned, but also spontaneous, occurring throughout the day and night as our thoughts turn to God. David writes that as he is lying upon his bed, he remembers God; as he wakes from sleep in the night, his thoughts turn to God. What was a mere bedroom became a sanctuary.

In our busy world today, it is good to know that simply turning our thoughts to God can transform our lives and allow us to experience God's presence in the midst of our activities. Driving a car, washing the dishes, or working in the garden can all become times of worship when we turn our thoughts to God, as David did during the watches of the night.

Dependence Brings Intimacy

As we grow in our dependence upon God, likewise we will grow in our intimacy with him. Jesus said, "Apart from me you can do nothing." He likened our dependence upon him to branches attached to a vine. If we do not remain attached, we will not survive.

David says to God, "My soul thirsts for you. . . . You are my help. . . . Your right hand upholds me." He recognizes his dependence upon God and draws even nearer as a result.

Before we leave David, let's look at a verse of another of the psalms.

One thing I ask of the Lord,
    this is what I seek:
that I may dwell in the house of the Lord
    all the days of my life,
to gaze upon the beauty of the Lord
    and to seek him in his temple
                        (Psalm 27:4).

If you could ask one thing of the Lord, what would it be? Long life, riches, fame, or maybe like Solomon you would ask for wisdom. What does the man after God's own heart desire? Intimacy with God. Dwelling in the house of the Lord—gazing upon the Lord's beauty. David expresses his desire to know God better to spend the time necessary to see the beauty of his Lord's character.

David's request in Psalm 27:4 always reminds me of the story of Martha and Mary. You remember how Mary sat at Jesus' feet listening to him while Martha prepared the home for the guests. When Martha complained that Mary wasn't helping her, Jesus answered her: "Martha, Martha, . . . you are worried and upset about many things, but only one thing is needed. Mary has chosen what is better, and it will not be taken from her" (Luke 10:41, 42).

Like David in the Old Testament, Mary of Bethany chose just one thing. The one thing that was needed. Intimacy with her Lord. Spending time with him. Listening to what he said.

There's a beautiful new chorus that is based on this text:

One thing is needful, O my Father,
One thing is needful, O my God;
That I sit at your feet and pour out my love,
This thing is needful, O my Lord![1]

Have you chosen the one thing that is needed—intimacy with God?

All too often we are more like Martha. Bustling about in efficient service. Coming to God with our prayer lists, but failing to see the value of sitting at Jesus' feet and simply enjoying his company. We will serve the Lord, but the motivation for that service is the time spent with Jesus.

I wonder if the church at Ephesus at the end of the first century ever identified with Martha? When Jesus spoke to the Ephesian church in Revelation 2, he commended them for their hard work, correct doctrine, and perseverance. Sounds a lot like Martha, doesn't it? But Jesus had a serious charge to level against the Ephesian church. They had lost their first love. I know that the text doesn't explain what that first love was, but I'm convinced that the first love of any Christian is Jesus himself. The first-century Ephesian Christians were a hard working, doctrinally correct group of passionless people who had fallen out of love with Jesus. No longer willing to simply sit at Jesus feet, they had to be up and about their business.

Sound like any church you know? Perhaps many of the churches you know? It is time for the church to repent of its busyness and prayerless activity and once again draw near to our Lord in love. God's promise is wonderful—draw near to me and I will draw near to you!

How to Get Started

When I first began preaching, my father told me that if I ended a sermon without telling the congregation how to do what I had been telling them they should do, I had failed in my task. Let me carry that advice over to the issue of intimacy with God in prayer. How can we grow in this area? How can we develop this passion for God? Here are some practical ideas to help us get started.

Spend Time With People in Love With God

Wouldn't it have been great to spend time with David as he worshiped and prayed? In addition to learning from

him, I think some of his passion for God would be conta-
gious. That kind of passion shows in the lives of those, like
David of old, who love the Lord, especially in the way they
pray and worship.

I've had the privilege of praying with a number of men
and women who have an intimate walk with the Lord. If I
know that any of these precious brothers or sisters are
going to be within driving distance, I try to get away to
spend some time with them in prayer. I always come away
refreshed and encouraged in my own quest for greater intimacy with God in prayer. You probably have someone in
your church from whom you could learn as you pray together.

Spend More Time With God

Reading this chapter alone will not give you a greater intimacy with God. The only thing that will do that is to actually spend more time with him. Spend time seeking to
know him—not just coming to him with our shopping lists.

On a purely human level, when we are growing in our
love for someone, we want to spend more and more time
with that person. It is the same with the Lord. The more we
know him, the more we love him, and the more we will
want to be with him.

Get to Know Him More in His Word

There's no better place to begin your walk of intimacy
with the Lord than in the pages of his Word. The Bible is
not just intended to give us facts and doctrine (though it
does that very well). Its purpose is to reveal God. Jesus crit-
icized the Pharisees because they studied the Bible, which
spoke of Jesus, but would not come to him.

We need to allow the Bible to teach us more about our
great God. Use the Bible as a place of prayer. As the Word
of God teaches you something about the nature of God,
stop and praise God for what you just learned about him.

Praying through the Bible should be one of the greatest experiences of your life.

Pray John 17:26

This is a prayer request that will change your life! At the close of his great high priestly prayer, Jesus prays to his Father on behalf of his disciples.

> I have made you known to them, and will continue to make you known in order that the love you have for me may be in them and that I myself may be in them.

How much does the Father love the Son? We cannot even begin to imagine, can we? Yet Jesus prayed that the love the Father has for him would be in us. Because this is a biblical prayer, from the very lips of our Lord, we know that it is a prayer according to God's will. And if we pray according to God's will, we know that he will answer that prayer.

What a great prayer for us to pray every day of our lives. "Father, I pray that you will help me to love Jesus as you love him, that your love for Jesus may be in me."

Imagine how our love for the Lord will grow as we pray this prayer and as God begins to answer the prayer he has literally written for us.

Here is one more prayer request to add to your list as you grow in intimacy with God. It comes from the apostle Paul—"I want to know Christ and the power of his resurrection and the fellowship of sharing in his sufferings, becoming like him in his death, and so, somehow, to attain to the resurrection from the dead" (Philippians 3:10, 11).

I want to know Christ! I want to experience the power of his resurrection in my life and know what it means to share in his sufferings. Can you imagine this request coming from the man who had experienced Christ's presence on the Damascus Road, who had been taught by the Lord in the desert for three years, who had been caught up into the third heaven and had experienced such revelation that he wasn't even allowed to speak of it! And still Paul prays, "I want to know Christ"

May that be our prayer as well!

Questions for Discussion

1. Why is the temptation to choose the important over the essential so strong? What safeguards can the church take against this?
2. What does it mean to "draw near to God"? How can you do it?
3. What does the author say is "the one thing that is needed"? Do you agree with his assessment? Why or why not?
4. Listed below are the five items the author suggests to develop intimacy with God. Which do you think is the most significant? Why? Which is the most difficult to achieve? Why? Which is easiest? Which is easiest to pretend to have? What is the danger of that?

   An expression of desire
   Remembrance of God's glory
   Expressions of praise
   Spontaneous times with God
   Dependence
5. Why was Mary praised when Martha did all the work? Isn't there something noble about ministering to the needs of others, as Martha did? Why was Mary's choice the right one on that particular occasion?
6. What can you do in the next three to five days to get started on developing intimacy with God? Will you do it?

---

[1]"One Thing Is Needful," Kirk Dearman. ©1981, Maranatha Music, (administered by The Copyright Company, Nashville, TN). All rights reserved. International copyright secured. Used by permission.

The Ultimate Strategy

Gary A. Barnes, Director of the Decade of Missions Project; Conference Coordinator of IVCF's Urbana 87 and the Love Europe Conference

The harvest is plentiful, but the laborers are few; pray therefore the Lord of the harvest to send out laborers into his harvest—Jesus.

Asking is the symbol of our desire. Some things God will not give until we want them enough to ask—E. Stanley Jones.

So also prayers for men are far more important than prayers for things because men more deeply concern God's will and the work of Jesus Christ than things—E.M. Bounds.

Recently I attended the annual meeting of the International Society for Frontier Missiology in Denver, Colorado. The papers, speeches, and presentations were overwhelming. The statistics were staggering. Evidence was presented of the great need to evangelize the megacities and the unreached or hidden people groups around the world. The purpose for the meeting was to discuss means, goals, and strategies for reaching the more than 65% of our earth's population who do not know Jesus Christ as their Lord and Savior—with the proposed deadline of A.D. 2000.

After the first day many of us were asking, "How do we translate these volumes of research and statistics into effective strategies to reach these unreached peoples of our world?" Billions of unreached people are without the Scriptures in their language or a church in their culture. Numerous ideas, suggestions, action plans, and strategies surfaced. But as we discussed which new strategies might be implemented in the coming decade to reach the lost, it became evident that we were missing something.

The members of this convention are faced with a great challenge, an overwhelming problem, but it has a simple, powerful solution. Jesus said, "The harvest is plentiful, but the laborers are few; *pray therefore* the Lord of the harvest, to send out laborers into his harvest" (Luke 10:2, RSV). He tells of the great challenge of a vast and endless harvest field. He also states that the problem is a lack of laborers to work in the harvest field. And he goes on to give us the ultimate or supreme strategy for solving this problem and meeting the challenge—prayer. Prayer is the strategy not only in response to the staggering evangelism and missions crisis of our time, but to literally all of the difficulties that we face today.

The Challenge: The Harvest Is Plentiful

Jesus said nearly two thousand years ago that the harvest was plentiful. The challenge is still before us today. Over 3.5 billion people on our planet do not know Jesus Christ and God's wonderful gift of grace and forgiveness. These people are part of 12,000 unreached people groups from around the world. These groups, according to the Adopt A People Clearinghouse, are deemed "unreached" for three reasons:

1. They have not had the gospel preached to them.

2. They do not have a church in their language or culture.

3. They do not have the Word of God translated into their language.

These groups make up over 65% of our earth's population. Some of the larger groups are the Chinese, Arabs, Hindus, Buddhists, and Animists.

There is more at stake than many care to imagine. The teachings of our Lord and the New Testament in general compel us to take the good news of Jesus to these people because the lost are still lost. To put many of these statistics into proper focus, we must remember that a second death and judgment await those who have never received Jesus as Lord and Savior over their lives. "Hell fire and brimstone" are still found from Matthew through the book of Revelation. Lost people face spending eternity without God the Father and our king Jesus. To be "cut off" and "cast out" into the darkness and the lake of fire that burns forever is a fate worse than cancer or AIDS.

The Problem: The Laborers Are Few

There were few laborers during the first century and there are still few laborers, despite an ever-increasing population. The number of people on earth, now over 5.5 billion, is going to continue to increase rapidly over the next twenty-five years. A vast number of cultures, hidden peoples, and unreached peoples are without missionaries or national Christians working among them. Of these 12,000 groups, many number only in the hundreds or thousands. Others number as many as one out of seven of the earth's population.

But the laborers are few, as these statistics show:

- Over 50% of the new missionary workers who go to the field will stay an average of only one four-year term.

- Over 80% of the present missionary force will work with groups who already have a significant population claiming to be Christian (which should be supporting themselves and reproducing disciples and churches without outside assistance).
- Less than 18% of the present missionary force work in the 55 least evangelized countries of the world (over 3 billion population).
- Over 50% of the present missionary force working around the world will reach retirement age or die over the next ten years.
- The average U.S. church gives only 2.5% of its budget to missions.

The problem of attrition is frightening to aware, involved churches and effective missions agencies. These obstacles are enormous. These statistics are genuine cause for grave concern. But these barriers are not insurmountable in light of Jesus' solution.

The Answer: "Pray Therefore"

Not only did Jesus do a great deal of teaching on the subject, he gave us examples of how, when, where, why, and what to pray. We find him praying for moments, hours, days, and even entire nights. We hear him urge his disciples to be faithful and persistent in prayer: "And will not God bring about justice for his chosen ones, who cry out to him day and night?" (Luke 18:7). Jesus prayed and wept over the city of Jerusalem and at the death of his friend Lazarus. He prayed and fasted for extended periods of time during temptation and difficulties. For Jesus, prayer was a way of life. He used prayer as his strategy to accomplish great things for God.

A recent event illustrating the power of prayer as a strategy are the circumstances developing in the former Soviet Union and Eastern Europe. For approximately seventy years Christians around the world have been praying that the misleading and misguided forces of Communism would fall. These same prayer warriors have been praying that the gospel might once again be proclaimed openly to the peoples throughout Eastern Europe and the Soviet Union. During the past few years the results of this decades-old strategy of prayer have begun to be seen. It was not Gorbachev, Reagan, or Bush who brought down the Berlin Wall or the Iron Curtain. It was not the TV evangelists or literature distribution or even the technology of satellite or radio. I believe the collapse of Communism, once seemingly invincible, was a direct response to the fervent, righteous prayers of faithful men and women following Jesus' teaching and strategy to "pray therefore."

Prayer was evident as Elijah's strategy for confronting and resolving the problems of life. In 1 Kings 17 we see Elijah using prayer as a strategy to raise the widow of Zarephath's son to life. The miracle that happened in that bedroom was an answer to the prayers of a righteous and faithful man of prayer.

In the subsequent chapter we read that Elijah again used prayer as his strategy to disgrace Baal and his prophets at Mount Carmel. He astutely suggested that both opposing parties build their individual altars and call on their respective gods to answer. This is how Elijah outlined the contest: "Then you will call on the name of your god, and I will call on the name of the Lord" (1 Kings 18:24).

From morning until evening, the 450 prophets of Baal prayed, chanted, sang, shouted, cut themselves, and fell prostrate on the ground. These attempts were futile. Then the moment of ultimate confrontation arrived. Elijah prayed. He did not hold a board meeting, conference, or seminar, nor did he call for a crisis planning meeting. He did not ask for a vote on how to go about accomplishing the task before him. He did not appoint a committee or recommend that everyone buy and read his latest book on being in tune with God. He did what the Scriptures have made plain both in the Old Testament and the New Testament. Elijah prayed. He just prayed, and the sacrifice was consumed! God was victorious, while the prophets of Baal looked foolish.

Prayer was Elijah's strategy for facing the circumstances that confronted him and God's people. James mentions Elijah's effective prayer strategy, telling how Elijah prayed for it not to rain and it did not rain! Three years later, when Elijah prayed for it to rain, God responded with rain. Elijah incorporated prayer as communication with God and as strategy for accomplishing God's will.

During the Thanksgiving season, I was in charge of a concert of prayer at a church in a university community. When the needs of the world were presented, we broke into small groups for prayer. One of the men in our group said, "It seems impossible! How could we ever reach the 3.5 billion lost by the year 2000?" A college student responded, "Don't forget Jesus did feed the five thousand with just five loaves and two fish in only a few hours." We all need to be reminded, from time to time, of our miracle-working, prayer-answering Lord God almighty! He can and will answer, but we first must ask.

As a missionary, I often wrestle with the heartbreaking burden of these lost peoples and the desire for the dawning of phenomenal strategies to reach them. In those times, I focus on the words of Jesus and understand that his command set forth the ultimate strategy. Here is Jesus' answer. Execute the strategy that is more powerful than all the technological smart bombs and nuclear weapons available to man. As I contemplate the task, Jesus' words, "Pray therefore; pray therefore," echo in my mind.

We do not need more committees, more satellites, more colleges, or more books on missions and evangelism. We do not need more seminars, workshops, conventions, or conferences. Instead, Jesus calls people to take seriously the ministry of prayer. Jesus yearns for more prayer warriors, prayer meetings, and prayer practicums! He aches for more meetings opened in prayer, focused on prayer, and concluded with prayer! Prayer as a strategy has too often been neglected, overlooked, or forgotten.

D. L. Moody wrote about the benefits of prayer as a strategy:

> Luther and his companions were men of such mighty pleading with God that they broke the spell of ages, and laid nations subdued at the foot of the cross. John Knox grasped all Scotland in his strong arms of faith and his prayers terrified tyrants. Whitefield, after much bold, faithful closet pleading, went to the devil's playground and took more than a thousand souls out of the paws of the lion in one day. . . . See a praying Wesley turn more than ten thousand souls to the Lord! Look at the praying Finney, whose prayers, faith, sermons and writings, have shaken this whole country and sent a wave of blessings through the churches on both sides of the sea.[1]

The list of these prayer warriors who held up the lost and the cause of evangelism and missions is compelling.

Recently we celebrated our son's fourth birthday. One of his gifts was a little car set with a matching village. As I glanced at the presumably simple instructions and noticed how few pieces there were to the kit, I decided to avoid the instructions in order to save time. After completing the assembly I realized I had three "extra" pieces. Two of the three seemed inconsequential but the third piece was essential to the stability of the kit. I had to disassemble the kit back to the stage where this piece was required. If only I had read and followed the simple instructions given on the sheet of paper accompanying the kit!

The work that we are doing for Christ Jesus could be strengthened and made easier, with greater and quicker results, if only we as brothers and sisters of our Lord's church took more seriously his simple, unembellished, foolproof directions to "pray therefore." No matter what the issue, situation, or problem, prayer is the first and best strategy. It is the alpha and omega to the Christian's way of living. It is the ultimate, supreme strategy for our lost world. Prayer is the key weapon to our spiritual warfare. No weapon or tool is as swift, capable, or effective. "I would rather stand against the cannons of the wicked than against the prayers of the righteous,"[2] said Thomas Lye. Our prayer life is the secret of becoming overcomers in all we do.

Often I have heard concerned brothers and sisters say, "I just don't know what I can do to reach my [brother, father, sister, mother, neighbor, friend] with the gospel." We are never excused from sharing our faith, but often the most strategic response we can have to accomplish that desire is to begin with a commitment to prayer. When a friend or relative seems impossible to reach, prayer should be the starting point in our desire for the gospel to penetrate this resistant individual's heart.

"Pray therefore." This is the ultimate weapon in reaching the world for Christ. Everyone can be involved in this strategy. That's the beauty of it! From the elderly widow, living on a meager fixed income, struggling to make ends meet each month; to the high school student, wrestling with the many compelling sermons and invitations to "follow"; to the college student, overwhelmed with loads of homework and mounting educational debts; to the young, harried family, raising three kids and mortgaged to the hilt to pay for the cars and house; to, finally, the couple who have seen their children marry and leave home and now have more time together than they did twenty years ago. What can all these people do today to make an impact on world evangelization? They can take seriously Jesus' command to pray.

"Pray therefore." Anyone, anywhere can respond. It is not an option, but a privilege, a responsibility, and a command. When we place the ultimate strategy at the center of our quiet times, prayer times, devotion times, and meditation times, world evangelization will begin to change us, our churches, and ultimately, the world.

More than 600 prayers are recorded in the Bible, without counting the Psalms. The Bible is a book of prayer and is about prayer warriors. Do you want to see revival in our land and see your congregation grow spiritually and numerically? Would it not be heart-stopping to see the Arab and Islamic world, the scattered Jews throughout the world, as well as the un-Christian millions of Asians and Malaysians (including the Chinese) fall on their knees in repentance and turn to the Lord Jesus Christ? And what about that relative, friend, or co-worker? Let's get to work as individuals and as congregations in restoring the strategy that Jesus gave for accomplishing world evangelization and, oh, so much more. "PRAY THEREFORE!"

Questions for Discussion

1. Have you ever before considered prayer to be the actual strategy for ministry, or have you always thought of prayer as supplemental to strategy—what you do when you cannot do anything else? What is the significance of viewing prayer as the "ultimate strategy"?
2. If prayer is, indeed, the ultimate strategy, then what is the place of other activity like preaching, planting churches, supporting missionaries, and the like?
3. How often do you pray for the billions of totally unreached peoples of the world—those with no Bibles, no churches, and no evangelists—"without hope and without God in the world" (Ephesians 2:12)? Can you organize a prayer group to pray for these people?
4. Do you think the shortage of laborers is worse today than when Jesus first expressed the concept? Why or why not? What can you do about it?
5. Do you agree with the author that the people groups who already have a significant population claiming to be Christian "should be supporting themselves and reproducing disciples and churches without outside assistance"? Why or why not?
6. If you agree with the author (see question #5), would you support a recall of all missionaries supported by your church to redeploy them into unreached areas?

7. How important do you think prayer was in the collapse of Communism in the former Soviet Union and in Europe? What does that suggest about the solution to other global problems?

8. The author says, "We do not need more committees, more satellites, more colleges, or more books on missions and evangelism. We do not need more seminars, workshops, conventions, or conferences. Instead, Jesus calls people to take seriously the ministry of prayer." Before you read another page of this book, take thirty minutes to pray for the lost.

9. Identify someone you know personally who does not know the Lord. Pray for this person daily.

[1]D.L. Moody, *Prevailing Prayer.* Chicago: Moody Press, p. 16.

[2]Thomas Lye, *The One Year Book of Personal Prayer.* Wheaton, IL: Tyndale House Publishers, 1991, p. 208.

My House Will Be Called a House of Prayer

Javonda J. Barnes, Missionary, known across Europe and the U.S. for her compassion, musical abilities, and prayer ministry

Structure. Time for others. Extensive Bible study. Regular quiet times. Long, in-depth conversations.

These words described days of a season in my life gone by. In those days I arose early, before punching the clock, for my routine, rarely-interrupted time of devotion and prayer. My after hours consisted of evening Bible studies and input with and from others.

These days gone by are my "B.K." days—Before Kids! In jest, I often reflect and wonder whether that "B.K." person was really me! Now my days are drastically different as a mother with three small children. I spend my waking hours meeting the varying needs of three precious souls. Each day does have structure and a plan, for without these my family's needs would not be met. Yet, inherent in the words "family" and "home" is the knowledge that often the most priceless of moments, significant in eternal terms, are the moments I have not structured or planned. These rich moments occur only as I balance necessity and spontaneity.

The adjustment from being employed outside my home to my present choice, "household watcher" (Proverbs 31:27), has required personal struggle. The struggle has not been in the obvious job description changes but with a personally conceived fallacy. This misunderstanding held that contributions of eternal value were somehow more rewarding if I were able to be personally involved. Praise God, I am grateful that I now have a clear, concrete understanding of the highest and most significant of ministries. That ministry is prayer. Prayer dispels the error that only "doing" can be significant. Prayer instead places significance on involvement in the ultimate battle between the spiritual forces of evil and God (Ephesians 6:12).

As warriors for God, we consider prayer to be the cadence of those marching in rhythm to the Great Commission (Acts 1:8). Jesus' parting words told of the battle "in Jerusalem, and in all Judea and Samaria, and to the ends of the earth" (Acts 1:8). Jesus spoke of the place where he stood (Jerusalem), the home region (Judea), the nearby region (Samaria), and the rest of the world.

It is hard to reconcile his command to go with the demands of one's role as wife and mother, which means not going. Can a commitment to these opposite actions reside in the same heart? Can a commitment exist that gives drive and passion for one's home (meals, laundry, diapers, and dealing with the flu), plus zeal and passion for one's "Jerusalem" (local social needs, education crises, political appointments, churches, and preachers)? Can a heart's commitment include these while radiating concern for one's "Judea" (governor, state officials, lottery, and abortion laws) and "Samaria" (unemployment, homelessness, teenage pregnancies, suicide machines, gay rights, and drug trafficking), while not neglecting "the ends of the earth" (3.5 billion lost souls, not to mention rain forests, the ozone layer, pollution, population, Russia, IRA, civil wars, and drought)? Yes. The commitment to Jerusalem,

Judea, Samaria, and the ends of the earth is the basis for the ministry of the home prayer warrior.

The wife and mother has the tremendous opportunity to commit herself to becoming a home prayer warrior. Although her role has physical restraints, it often leaves her heart free to do spiritual battle for the Great Commission. What a beautiful, powerful sight—busy, committed hands with a boundless heart! This mother heart, with its immeasurable attributes of perseverance and faith, is moldable material for the significant ministry of prayer. God can nurture this heart, harnessing these attributes, resulting in an ability for the home prayer warrior to see the world as one's home as well as one's prayer responsibility.

The attributes involved in the act of mothering have motivating parallels with the ministry of prayer. For example, prayer requires tenacity. So does mothering. We are determined in our commitment to contribute to the kingdom of Heaven. We persevere even when the odds seem unlikely, as in prayer for the resistant harvest of the Islamic world (Luke 10:5-13). Prayer is serving others. This, too, is a clear definition of mothering. Likewise, prayer is daily choosing to look out for the best interests of another and being consumed by thoughts of others' needs (Philippians 1:3, 9-11; 2:3-5). Prayer is commitment for the future; we know that our children's futures result from our mothering today. Prayer, like mothering, requires our heart's best energies. It is a behind-the-scenes, less-visible ministry. This prayer ministry, as Jesus taught in Matthew 6:5, 6, begins in our prayer closets where no one sees but the heavenly Father!

To increase our availability for this behind-the-scenes ministry as a home prayer warrior, we must honestly evaluate our current prayer awareness. How do I respond to situations and thoughts as they arise in my day? Do I respond in prayer to situations, or do my days pass in defeat as I fail to seek heavenly power? Do I succumb to doubt and despair stimulated by specific thoughts? Do I spend long periods of time harboring critical thoughts of others? Or do I, in my desire to bring every thought captive to the lordship of Jesus Christ (2 Corinthians 10:5), respond to thoughts as being promptings for prayer?

Your desire as a prayer warrior is for prayer to become an involuntary reflex in response to the challenges of the day. But this involuntary prayer reflex does not develop without assimilating the words, "I want to pray," and, "I must pray" into your response to every situation or thought. These words help us to follow Paul's exhortation to "pray continually" (1 Thessalonians 5:17). And these words, when nurtured, can permeate our lives to the point that mundane tasks like ironing become anticipated, effective, and extended times of prayer. Like many tasks, ironing requires physical involvement and yet it leaves one's mind free to be engaged in spiritual battle through prayer. So thoughts of individuals, situations, or crises can be utilized as an agenda for prayer. How wonderful to weave prayer into every thought and deed!

Think through a typical day's sights and happenings. Perhaps as you awake, having enjoyed the blessing of a good night's rest (Psalm 4:8), your heart can turn to those people you know who are experiencing the pain of the inability to sleep due to a stressful family situation. As you prepare the morning breakfast, your heart can be moved to intercede on behalf of the people of Russia, whose daily food is not a certainty (James 2:15). As your children prepare for school, you sense God's prompting to pray for their teachers, administrators, and school personnel as well as for your friends and their children's school day needs (Philippians 1:3). Often we are aware of a friend whose child faces a specific battle.

What happens in your heart as you stand waiting in the grocery checkout line and your eye catches the headlines of newspapers or periodicals? Instead of succumbing to doubt, frustration, or fear, quickly turn your thoughts into prayer regarding what you have seen. What do you do with your thoughts when you walk down the street and are aware that the teenagers you see are engaging in activities of darkness, unaware of consequential dangers? Begin to intercede for them. As we pray, we are recognizing our inability to "do" anything about a particular situation, and yet, we are also saying that we believe God is capable and that he loves and understands each person.

We need to recognize that every act of meeting a need or performing a chore can be seen or utilized as a prompting to pray. For a mother, some of our longest hours are those spent comforting an ill child. But the prayer warrior resists the temptation to spend this time in increasing frustration. Instead, she knows that this time can be doubly blessed as she nurses the child and also turns her heart's thoughts from frustration to the furtherance of the kingdom of Heaven. If the illness involves sleepless nights, we are able to reflect David's feelings that the night brings thoughts of God (Psalm 16:7), and we are beckoned to Heaven's throne on behalf of others. An illness may prompt thoughts of individuals, communities, and countries in various parts of the world whose people daily face horrible physical suffering without adequate medical intervention. Again, we see our prayers as reflecting our heart's concern for our "Jerusalem," but further being moved for our "Judea" and "Samaria," continuing until we encompass "the ends of the earth."

When in doubt as to what is best to pray, effective prayers reflect Jesus' concern: "Thy kingdom come" (Matthew 6:10). We do not need to be consumed by concern over our inability to frame impressive, power-packed prayers—the issue is the response of our hearts. How precious to God that our hearts plead on behalf of others, "Thy kingdom come." This simple prayer engulfs every creation's needs. For example, when you hold a small child whose home does not have the influence of biblical truth and you are feeling overwhelmed, a fitting prayer to whisper on his behalf is, "Thy kingdom come. Please send laborers to touch this home" (Luke 10:2). Without the avenue of prayer and the comfort it provides, the ills of our present day would be genuine causes of doubt, fear, and despair (Luke 21:34-36). But we are not people of darkness; we are of the light. We do not give ourselves over to doubts or fears or despair; we simply bring all of these before the throne of grace (Philippians 4:6, 7) pleading, "Thy kingdom come."

If we desire to be effective world prayer warriors, it is necessary to supply our hearts with missions information so we have missions thoughts. Begin to read as much missions-related materials as you can get your hands on. A newspaper or a credible periodical can also be a good guide for world prayer needs. Mothers of newborns should feel free to read only the opening paragraphs and the concluding summaries of articles! Since mothers are often restricted to specific places, be strategic and have applicable materials available within arm's reach—under the high chair or near the rocking chair. Think about those critical places where your body is occupied, yet your heart and mind are free and available for prayer. (If your children are older, share insights from the reading and the passion of your heart for the world. These can be timely, superb seeds planted in young hearts.)

Be creative in your approach to grow in your love for God's world. Recognize your personal strengths as well as your limitations, and work within these. For mothers of infants, having time in which to stimulate one's mind and experience a sense of accomplishment might seem an unrealistic dream. Nonetheless, there are moments to be grasped and directed into prayer. For me, prayer complements a personal growth challenge to increase my geographical knowledge. It grieves me to admit that prior to living in Europe, I probably would have been unable to locate Eastern Europe on the map!

Given the fact that your desire to be a home prayer warrior is a commitment between you and God, there are no limits to the creativity you might employ. For example, depending on the number of rooms in your home, an idea might be to see each room as representing certain continents. As you enter a room, pray for the nations of that continent. Perhaps after praying for continents, certain rooms might represent specific resistant people groups. The ideas are limitless! As our hearts respond with willingness, God provides the food for prayer—that's the beauty of it!

Perhaps the greatest challenge will be to continue in prayer over the long term. Every decision for growth is like the onset of a trip, whether the journey is three feet or 7,000 miles. Both trips begin with the same decision—taking the first step! Such is true for the development of a prayer warrior. We must respond as did the disciples when stirred by Jesus' clear dedication to prayer. They asked Jesus to teach them to pray. They desired to pray more, but their flesh was weak and too easily betrayed their desire (Luke 11:1, Matthew 26:41).

Deciding to make prayer a more integral element of your life is commendable, but follow through is another matter! As with all decision for change, it is imperative to reinforce that choice with accountability, perhaps by telling a friend of your decision to begin. (If your heart's motivation is pure, God will be faithful to bring the help and encouragement you need.) Ask this friend to remind you of your decision and tell her you would like her prayers in maintaining your commitment. This maintenance system will be especially sweet as you share in victories won by persevering in prayer.

Prayer should be our response to absolutely every situation. Every thought should be taken captive and funneled into prayer. We are committed to praying on behalf of our "Jerusalem," "Judea," "Samaria," and "the ends of the earth." For our redeemed, free hearts, prayer is the first response to Jesus' marching orders.

While marching to the cadence of the Great Commission, a mother at home—consumed by meeting never-ending practical needs—must recognize she is there just for a season of her life. How glorious for a mother to complete that season fully satisfied, without any regrets, and immeasurably charged, having lived those days with her heart on its knees and having knowledge of tremendous victories won through prayer.

Questions for Discussion

1. The author says, "Prayer dispels the error that only 'doing' can be significant." Where do you think we got that error in the first place? How can we prevent it from continuing?

2. The Lord's command to go to Jerusalem, Judea, Samaria, and the ends of the earth is applied to mothers, whose range of personal influence is much more limited. What are your Jerusalem, Judea, and Samaria? What are you doing about them?

3. What routine tasks do you perform each day that requires little concentration so that your mind could be occupied in prayer?

4. The author notes that prayer is a behind-the-scenes ministry. Does human pride prevent us from accepting the ministry of prayer because it offers no recognition?

5. Disturbing thoughts can be cause for worry or, as the author suggests, prompting for prayer. How can you discipline yourself to choose the latter?

6. In what way is "Thy kingdom come" an appropriate prayer for any situation? Think of one or two situations about which you need to pray that prayer now. Do it.

7. The author suggests a stay-at-home mom could think of a different continent for each room in the house and pray for the lost on those continents upon entering each room. Suggest a similar concept for your own situation.

8. Mrs. Barnes says, "Prayer should be our response to absolutely every situation." Is it for you? What can you do to be sure it is? How can the church work together to make that true of the body?

Deepening Your Prayer Life

Ward Patterson, Professor of Communication and Campus Ministry at Cincinnati Bible College; Former Campus
Minister at Indiana University

Prayer is the language of a holy relationship. It is the language of love, adoration, friendship, clarification, honesty, truth, dependence, longing, warmth, caring, understanding, submission, remembrance, and unity.

Prayer is the language of holy communion. It is the language of knowing and being known, of remembering and envisioning, of trusting and comforting. It is the language of presence, power, and peace.

Prayer is the language of awareness. It is the language of awe, thanksgiving, repentance, sorrow, hope, truth, pain, anguish, acceptance, obedience, grace, renewal, and faith.

Prayer is the language of celebration. It is the language of joy, delight, excitement, adventure, fulfillment, gladness, exuberance, freedom, contentment, happiness, and fun.

Like all any language, prayer must be learned. We learned our native language by listening and imitating, studying and practicing, using and exercising.

When we learned our language, we first heard words from our parents and teachers and tried to say them as we heard them. Gradually we came to express thoughts. We went to school and were taught the rules of the language we already spoke. We learned grammar, spelling, and punctuation. Our world broadened as we began to enjoy reading and writing and discovered the wonders of literature. We continue in a lifelong endeavor to know and use language well.

When I first began to pray in public, I prayed as I had heard others pray. I imitated prayers I had heard in my home and my church. Later I began to study the prayers of the Bible. I studied Scriptures relating to prayer and learned to recognize the elements of praise, petition, intercession, confession, and contrition. The quest continues as I seek to deepen my understanding and practice of the language of prayer.

In prayer we are all beginners. Even if we have advanced beyond the "Da-da" stage, we are aware that we are often inconstant, distracted, unfocused, inattentive, insincere, selfish, and empty in our prayer lives. Sometimes, to use the language analogy further, we are like a person who has studied a foreign language from books and knows all the vocabulary and the rules of the language but cannot speak the language. We study prayer and talk about the importance of prayer, but we do not pray.

How can we become versed in prayer? Peter, writing to Christians during a time of terrible persecution, wrote, "The end of all things is near. Therefore be clear minded and self-controlled so that you can pray" (1 Peter 4:7). He seems to be saying that there is an urgency about prayer, that there is a mind-set for prayer, and that there is a discipline in prayer.

Recognizing the Urgency of Prayer

We live in an increasingly harried and hurried society. Time is viewed as our most valued commodity. Americans

define themselves by their activities, articulate their importance by their complaints of overwork, and exhaust themselves in the endless pursuit of fulfillment. We could pray,
we tell ourselves, if we could just get the time . . . if we
could just find a time when the family was all together . . .
if we could just work it into our schedule on a regular
basis. But Peter reminds his hearers, and us, that we don't
have time not to pray. Prayer is not a useful, discretionary
add-on for the super-Christian, it is the very life of the
Christian faith. Whether Christ should return or whether
we should cease to live, time is too short to neglect prayer.

Developing a Mind-set for Prayer

Peter urges Christians to be "clear minded" in order to
pray. The Greek here suggests that the Christian should be
of a steady mind, of a sane mind, of a discerning and bal-
anced mind. William Barclay observed,

> The great characteristic of sanity is that it sees things in their
> proper proportions; it sees what things are important and what
> things are not important; it is not swept away by sudden and
> capricious and transitory enthusiasms; it is prone neither to
> unbalanced fanaticism nor to unrealizing indifference. It is
> only when we see the affairs and the activities of earth in the
> light of eternity that we see them in their proper proportions
> and their proper importances. It is when God is given His
> proper place that all things take their proper places.[1]

Practicing Discipline in Prayer

The word translated "self-controlled" in the NIV has the
idea of being sober, sensible, and in control. It is the opposite of being drunk, out of control, erratic, unpredictable,

muddled, or befuddled. This implies a certain seriousness about prayer, a sense of its nature and importance, a sensible approach to the development of a deep and meaningful prayer life.

The focus on prayer can be so easily blurred. We need clarity of mind and spirit if we are to pray as we ought. It is very easy to make prayer the end in itself rather than seeing it as a means to the end of knowing and pleasing God.

Like an orator who becomes enamored with the sound of his own voice and struts his eloquence in order to call attention to his superior mastery of words, we can, if we are not careful, become more excited about prayer than about the God with whom we communicate through our prayers.

The writer to the Hebrews wrote, "Without faith it is impossible to please God, because anyone who comes to him must believe that he exists and that he rewards those who earnestly seek him" (Hebrews 11:6). Belief in the existence of God and belief in the providence of God are key elements for both faith and prayer. A recent Gallup poll reported that 94% of American adults say they believe in God, but one wonders what kind of God many of them believe in. The God of the Christian faith is a God who created the universe from nothing (Hebrews 11:3). Paul described him as eternal, immortal, invisible, and wise (1 Timothy 1:17).

Not only does he exist, but he is involved in his world. He is not an impersonal "first cause" or mindless, uninvolved "universal life principle." He is not a distant "highest good," or an abstract "ground of all being." He is intimately at work in our world, looking out for those who earnestly seek him. The prayerful seeker finds the benefits of God in the ordinary and the extraordinary events of life.

Developing an Attitude of Expectancy

We live in a utilitarian society. We Americans like to see results—tangible, measurable, dramatic results. I recently ran across a book written in the late 1950's. It was entitled *The Power of Prayer on Plants.* Its author, a certain Franklin Loehr, set out to prove scientifically the power and efficacy of prayer. In the front of the book was the announcement, "In what may be proved one of the most important scientific documents of the 20th Century, Dr. Franklin Loehr proves beyond doubt that loving prayer will make your plants grow. . . ."

In a straightforward manner the author reported his experiments. Using 27,000 seeds and 100,000 measurements, he proved that those seeds that were prayed for grew over 50% more than those that were not prayed for. An experiment in England confirmed his prayer research. A 12-acre plot was planted with carrots, and people 300 miles away prayed for the carrots. They produced a 20.5% larger carrot crop with more marketable carrots than the un-prayed-for control acres located near the people praying, it was claimed. Loehr experimented with prayer both for or against growth in corn shoots, African violets, wheat seeds, ivy, and silkworms. He concluded that the effects of prayer on plants was certain proof of the power of prayer. It did not, he noted, seem to make much difference in the results whether the people praying had a biblical or an eastern mystical concept of God.

Rev. Loehr's experiments derive more from occultism than from Christianity. We may fault his motivation and his methodology, but we cannot fault his hypothesis— prayer makes a difference.

I sincerely doubt if James had carrots in mind when he wrote, "The prayer of a righteous man is powerful and effective" (James 5:16). Jesus instructs us, "Ask and it will be given to you; seek and you will find; knock and the door will be opened to you. For everyone who asks receives; he who seeks finds; and to him who knocks, the door will be opened" (Matthew 7:7, 8). Further, he says, "If you remain in me and my words remain in you, ask whatever you wish, and it will be given you. This is to my Father's glory, that you bear much fruit, showing yourselves to be my disciples" (John 15:7, 8).

There are almost unbelievable promises associated with sincere, constant, patient, believing, trusting prayer. Yet we often pray more in desperate hope than in confident faith.

God "rewards those who earnestly seek him." Prayer does change things. Sometimes my prayers change my circumstances, and sometimes they change my focus, and sometimes they change my attitude.

God's lovingkindness, mercy, and willingness to concern himself with us is a great wonder. God hates sin, yet he loves me, an abject sinner. It is only through the blood of Christ that I can draw near to this holy God (Hebrews 10:19-22).

There is a tendency here, as we listen to the sweeping promises connected to prayer, to view prayer as a simple, selfish transaction. I tell God what I want and he gives me what I want, regardless of my obedience, regardless of my motives, regardless of the purposes of his kingdom. Prayer becomes my letter to Santa, or my coin in the vending machine of goodies, or my rub of Aladdin's lamp. I'm reminded of the child who, in prayer, listed all the things he wanted God to do. Then, after his "Amen," he added a postscript: "Say, God, is there anything you want?" We deepen our prayer lives, I think, when we become more concerned about what God wants than what we want.

Yet we need to remember that God delights in showering us with good. Jesus said, "Which of you, if his son asks for bread, will give him a stone? Or if he asks for a fish, will give him a snake? If you, then, though you are evil, know how to give good gifts to your children, how much more will your Father in heaven give good gifts to those who ask him!" (Matthew 7:9-11).

This cannot be reduced to a simple "name it and claim it" formula. A good father does not indulge his children by giving them everything their whims desire, but he does look out for their good and express his love in generosity.

James suggests that while we ask God for those things we want, we also examine our motives to be sure that what we long for is not desired merely to satisfy our worldly pleasures (James 4:1-3).

Developing a Vocabulary of Praise

I believe that one of the most lacking elements of our prayer lives is the area of praise and adoration of God. It seems to me, as I pray and share in the prayers of others, that we have the most difficulty in wording our appreciation for who God is. Perhaps it is because we do not commonly use this language in our human relationships. We are used to asking others for things we need. We are accustomed to asking others to forgive us. We often speak of the needs of others as we talk with one another. But to speak of the exalted attributes of mere humans is to exceed the bounds of propriety and reality.

The Psalms are worthy of our careful study. They are the inspired writings instructing us in how to talk to and about God. They are filled with expressions of praise and adoration, recognition of the power and the presence of God, and awareness of the providence and mercy of God. The Psalms give us examples from which we can learn— examples of the God-saturated mind, of the God-longing heart, of the God-fearing soul. We need both to study and emulate the Psalms. We need to pray the Psalms and use them to help us develop a mind-set of love and appreciation for God.

As an example, here is a prayer that is based on Psalm 138:

Lord, I will praise you with exuberance.
   I want my heart and mind to be involved
      as well as my tongue and lips.
   My spirit is lifted up in song
      as I contemplate your greatness.

There is no other object or being worthy of my praise.
   You are the focus of my adoration.
      I love to gather with the faithful to praise you.
   Your name is high above any other name
      in heaven or on earth.

Your Word is true and holy forever.
   Your love and faithfulness
      are my constant contemplation.
   I bow my head and heart to you,
      O great and wonderful God.

You hear my prayers.
   You give me strength to meet each day.
      You make me secure and resolute.
         You intervene on my behalf.

O that all people would praise you!
   O that people of influence would exalt your name!
      O that people everywhere would listen for your words,
         and sing songs of your marvelous ways,
            and proclaim the news of your great glory.

You are not influenced by reputations,
   social standing,
      or success.
You have a special love for the lowly and the needy.
   In my times of trouble,
      you preserve me.
In my times of fear and impotency,
   You overcome my foes and lead me to victory.

O Lord, fulfill your purposes for me.
   Hold me close and wrap me in your everlasting love.
      Stay close beside me.
         Keep my eyes on you every moment of every day.

                           AMEN.[2]

Expanding the Horizons of Our Prayers

Much of our praying seems to focus on the temporal and the immediate, the physical and the material. These are certainly worthy of God's and our concern. But I seem to need help in focusing on the things of God's ultimate concern rather than my immediate desires. In the Sermon on the Mount, Jesus instructed his followers to pray, "Your kingdom come, your will be done on earth as it is in heaven" (Matthew 6:10). We need to deepen our prayers for the kingdom and the carrying out of God's will. The praying of Scripture has proved to be a help to me in this area. As an example, here is a prayer prompted by 2 Corinthians 1:1-11:

Our Father God, I thank you
    for the grace and peace you alone can give.
        I thank you for the forgiveness,
            renewal,
                unmerited love,
                    patience,
                        lovingkindness,
                        and mercy
                            that you bestow without measure.

I thank you for reconciling me to you
    and quieting the turmoil within me.
I thank you for your assurances,
    Your providence,
        Your provision.
Help me to trust your will for my life.
    Help me to respond faithfully to your call.

I thank you for the church for which Christ died.
    I thank you for all the saints
        who faithfully serve you throughout the world.
    I thank you for the apostolic teaching
        that instructs and enlightens us.
    I praise you for the comfort you bring
        to the distresses of my life.

I praise you, God, for you are the Father
    of my Lord Jesus Christ.

You are the Father of compassion,
  comfort,
    salvation,
      endurance,
        hope,
          resurrection,
            deliverance,
              help,
                gracious favor,
                  and answered prayer.

You lift me up when I am down,
  strengthen me when I am weak,
    and console me when I am depressed.
You heal my hurts.
  You are generous with your comfort.
  Whatever is wrong, you make right.

You produce patient endurance in my life, day by day,
  by the things I am called upon to endure.
With the shared experience of suffering
  comes the shared experience of triumph.
My hope in you never falters.
  You are ever near.
  You are with me in every circumstance.

When hardships come,
  I learn to rely more firmly on you.
When pressure bears down on me
  and I feel as if sentenced to death,
    I learn that I need you to sustain me.
Help me not to rely on myself but to rely on you.
  All power is yours.
    Nothing is beyond your strength,
      not even death.

You have delivered me from death
  and from every other thing that would threaten me.

There is nothing to come that need cause me alarm.
You are my help and my hope.
Deliver me from evil.
Listen to my prayers.
Accept my thanksgiving.
Grant me your favor.
Give heed to the intercessions of your people.

AMEN.

Covenanting With Others in Prayer

Prayer can be solitary or communal, private or public, spontaneous or studied. I have found regular prayer times with a few close friends to be extremely helpful in deepening my prayer life. Jesus said, "Again, I tell you that if two of you on earth agree about anything you ask for, it will be done for you by my Father in heaven. For where two or three come together in my name, there am I with them" (Matthew 18:19, 20).

When I was at the University of Indiana, we in the speech department developed a small prayer group. We established a closeness with one another and with God that was a strength to us in the daily demands of our studies. In my campus ministry, I was in a prayer partnership with a fellow campus minister. We prayed together about our separate works, and I shared in his vision for a mission to Oxford, England, where he and his wife now serve. In my new teaching ministry, I look forward to my weekly prayer time with two fellow faculty members. Their faith and consistency in Christ have helped me to go deeper in my walk with him. Wherever we may be there is someone else with whom we can enter into a partnership of regular prayer. If you have not found such a person or persons, you may want to pray that God will lead you to an appropriate partnership of prayer.

Enjoying God

It is a humbling thing to try to write about deepening our prayer lives.

Who am I, Lord, to instruct others when I have so much to learn? Father, help me to live what I know, to seek you early and late, in good times and in bad, in strength and in weakness, in happiness and in sorrow. Help me to experience the meaning of prayer as well as understand the meaning of prayer. Help me to be dissatisfied with shallowness, slothfulness, and sham.

Lord, in the busyness of today, help me to speak the language of love with my thoughts, my mouth, and my actions.

Give me a longing for you, a joy in you, and a trust in you.

I seek to add my voice to the chorus of celestial beings that constantly surround you in adoration and praise. You are my source of enlightenment, my wellspring of joy, my fountainhead of understanding, my giver of righteousness, my supplier of strength. You fill my life will all that I need. You protect me from danger. You watch out for my interests. You direct my path by your light.

Dear God, I was created for fellowship with you. Let me enter into your presence with infectious joy. Let me seek your counsel and know your wisdom. Bind up my wounds, resolve my dilemmas, and protect me from evil. Through Jesus Christ.

AMEN.

Questions for Discussion

1. In what ways is learning to pray like learning a foreign language?
2. What is the "urgency" of prayer? In our time-frantic society, why has that point seemingly been lost? Do you think recovering the urgency of prayer would help us

cope with the time demands each of us faces? Why or why not?

3. What is significant about the "mind-set" for prayer? How can one develop such a mind-set?
4. Why is discipline required for an effective prayer life?
5. The author says we need to develop an attitude of expectancy? What should we be expecting? Why?
6. How does focusing on how God has answered prayers in the past help us in our present prayers?
7. How does a "vocabulary of praise" enrich one's prayers?
8. Why is it so easy to dwell only on the temporal and the material in our prayers? If we would go beyond the temporal and material, about what would we pray?
9. In what ways does covenanting with others to pray help strengthen one's prayer life?
10. Of all the author's suggestions, which do you need most to implement? Which has already helped enrich your prayers?

    Recognizing the urgency of prayer
    Developing a mind-set for prayer
    Practicing discipline
    Developing an attitude of expectancy
    Developing a vocabulary of praise
    Expanding the horizons of our prayers
    Covenanting with others

11. Can you say you truly "enjoy God"? How can a deeper prayer life help you to enjoy his fellowship more?
12. Share the Prayer Covenant on page 111 with another believer. Covenant together to pray regularly for personal renewal, awakening in the churches, and for laborers.

---

[1]William Barclay, *The Letters of James and Peter. (The Daily Study Bible Series.)* Philadelphia: Westminster Press, 1960, p. 298.

[2]Ward Patterson, *Into His Love.* Denver: Accent Books, 1988, pp. 91, 92.

Overview of the Format

A Concert of Prayer

Following the pattern of concerts of prayer over the past 250 years, as well as prayer movements emerging nation-wide and world-wide today, here is one model of a format for a two-hour Concert of Prayer. The approach provides not only a satisfying experience during a prayer concert, but can be adapted for use in a variety of churches, fellowships and ministries so that the vision and ministry of united prayer may spread.

Celebration (15 minutes)

- •Praise in hymns and choruses, focused on awakening and mission
- •Reports of God's answers to prayers offered up during previous concerts

•Prayers of praise for God's faithfulness, for his kingdom, for his Son

Preparation (20 minutes)

•Welcome to the concert!
•Overview: Why are we here?
•Biblical perspectives on what we're praying toward
(i.e., awakening, mission)
•Preview of the format
•Teaming-up in partners and in huddles

Dedication (5 minutes)

•Commitment: to be servants through prayer and to be
used in answer to our prayers
•Thanksgiving: for the privilege of united prayer and for
those with whom we unite
•Invitation for Christ to lead the concert and to pray
through us
•Hymn of praise

Seeking of Fullness/Awakening in the Church (30 minutes)

•In partners—for personal revival
•In huddles—for awakening in our local churches and
ministries
•As a whole—for awakening in the church world-wide
•Pause to listen to our Father
•Chorus

Seeking for Fullfilment/Mission Among the Nations (30 minutes)

•In partners—for personal ministries
•In huddles—for outreach and mission in our city or
campus

- As a whole—for world evangelization
- Pause to listen to our Father
- Chorus

Testimonies: What Has God Said to Us Here? (10 minutes)

- On fullness (awakening)
- On fulfillment (mission)

Grand Finale (10 minutes)

- Offering ourselves to be answers to our prayers and also to live accordingly
- Prayer for God's empowerment in our own lives for ministry
- Prayer for prayer movements locally and world-wide
- Offering praise to the Father who will answer our concerts of prayer
- Leave to watch and serve "in concert"

Seven Themes in Concerted Prayer

I. *Preparation*
- Prelude (15 minutes beforehand)
- Worship and praise (10 minutes)
- Welcome and introductions (7 minutes)

II. *Biblical Vision—A Call to the Hope* (20 minutes)

III. *Concerted Prayer Toward the Hope* (1 hour and 35 minutes)
- An invitation for Christ to lead us by the Holy Spirit (3 minutes)
- A. Rejoice
- B. Repent

C. Resist
D. Restore
E. Release
F. Receive
G. Recommit

IV. *Grand Finale*
- Celebration (13 minutes)
- Benediction (2 minutes)
- Postlude (played as people leave)

An offering may be included after the welcome or as part of the time of recommitment. In either case, additional music may take place during the offering.

Resources on Prayer

Bryant, David. *Concerts of Prayer.* Regal Books, 1984.
A stirring call for the church to come together to pray for awakening and the task of world evangelization.

Bryant, David. *Operation Prayer II.* Concerts of Prayer, International, 1990. A 36-page booklet detailing steps for conducting a Concert of Prayer in your church or community.

Duewel, Wesley L. *Mighty Prevailing Prayer.* Zondervan, 1991. Prayer veteran Leonard Ravenhill calls this work "Superb ...priority reading ...a desktop encyclopedia! A lifetime manual for the serious student of the prayer life."

Duewel, Wesley L. *Touch the World Through Prayer.* Zondervan, 1986. This classic work on intercession shows the importance of prayer to the success of evangelistic and mission efforts.

Hunt, T.W. *Church Prayer Ministry Manual*. Nashville: The Sunday School Board of the Southern Baptist Convention, 1981. A Southern Baptist manual containing many great ideas for developing the prayer ministry of the local church.

Hunt, T.W., and Catherine Walker. *Disciples Prayerlife Notebook*. Nashville: The Sunday School Board of the Southern Baptist Convention, 1988. One of the best Bible studies available on the complete prayer life. This extensive notebook was prepared especially for the Southern Baptist Convention, but will be appreciated by all praying Christians.

Prayers That Prevail. Victory House, 1990.
Here is a "believer's manual of prayers" compiled from the Word of God. Addressing more than 100 topics of vital concern to every believer, this is a tremendous biblical tool for building a more effective prayer life!

Shepherd, Glenn. *Global Prayer Strategy*. International Prayer Ministries, 1989. A 34-page booklet prepared by the Intercession Working Group of the Lausanne Committee for World Evangelization, which maps out a prayer strategy to undergird the task of world evangelization.

Vander Griend, Alvin. *Passion and Power in Prayer*. Church Development Resources. New 3-tape video course.
A practical, biblical course with individual notebooks designed to increase the number of prayer warriors in your church. Especially good for teaching people to pray together in small groups.

Vander Griend, Alvin. *The Praying Church Sourcebook*. Church Development Resources, 1990. A complete prayer program for your church. This reproducible notebook contains 27 prayer strategies to help you tap into the tremendous power that prayer can bring to your church.

All of the above materials can be ordered through:

Missions Prayer Ministry
Box 301
Kansas, IL 61933
(217) 948-5131

Prayer Bibliography

Billheimer, Paul. *Destined to Overcome.* Christian Literature Crusade, Inc., 1982.

Bounds, E.M. *The Necessity of Prayer.* Baker, 1976, or Whitaker House, 1984.

Bounds, E.M. *Power Through Prayer.* Several publishers.

Bright and Jennings, eds. *Unleashing the Power of Prayer.* Moody Press, 1989.

Brother Lawrence. *Practice of the Presence of God.* Revell.

Bryant, David. *Concerts of Prayer.* Concerts of Prayer, International, 1990.

Cho, Paul Y. Prayer: *Key to Revival.* Word Books, 1987.

Dawson, Joy. *Intimate Friendship With God.* Revell, 1986.

Duewel, Wesley. *Touch the World Through Prayer.* Zondervan, 1986.

Duewel, Wesley. *Mighty Prevailing Prayer.* Zondervan, 1991.

Hallesby, O. *Prayer.* Augsburg, 1959.

Hayford, Jack. *Prayer Is Invading the Impossible.* Bridge Publishers, 1977.

Miller, Calvin. *The Table of Inwardness.* InterVarsity, 1984.

Murray, Andrew. *The Prayer Life.* Whitaker House, 1981.

Ravenhill, Leonard. *Revival God's Way.* Bethany House, 1983.

Ravenhill, Leonard. *Revival Praying.* Bethany House, 1962.

Rice, John R. *Prayer: Asking & Receiving.*

Smith, Chuck. *Effective Prayer Life.* Word for Today, 1980.

Smith, Hannah Whiteall. *The Christian's Secret of a Happy Life.* Several publishers.

White, John. *Daring to Draw Near.* InterVarsity, 1977.

A Prayer Covenant

I. Pray for a Personal Renewal

All of us are imperfect in our walks and in our prayer lives. Personal worship needs to be strengthened. A deeper sense of mission to fulfill the Great Commission is appropriate for every member of the body of Christ.

II. Pray for an Awakening in the Churches

Some congregations are growing and reaching out, but every congregation can do more about reaching its full potential for service. Some congregations are lukewarm, and some are stone cold dead. Awakening to the Great Commission is a need in all the churches.

III. Pray for Laborers (Luke 10:2)

The result can be worldwide evangelization!